REGULATE TO
RISE

Regulate to Rise
The Hidden Key to Powerful Leadership and Personal Peace

Sam Willing

©2025 All Rights Reserved. No portion of this book may be reproduced, stored in a retrieval system, or transmitted in any form or by any means—electronic, mechanical, photocopy, recording, scanning, or other—except for brief quotations in critical reviews or articles without the prior permission of the author.

Published by Game Changer Publishing

Illustrations by Ali Willing

Paperback ISBN: 978-1-969372-35-3
Hardcover ISBN: 978-1-969372-36-0
Digital ISBN: 978-1-969372-37-7

www.GameChangerPublishing.com

To my husband:
Your steadiness, laughter, and quiet strength have held me in every season. There is no one I'd rather do this life with, and I will be eternally grateful to God for putting us together.

To my children:
Thank you for witnessing the unglamorous and holy work of my healing. You are my greatest teachers and my proudest legacy.

And to the leaders, the ones doing the deep, courageous work to bring humanity back into leadership: May you continue to lead not from perfection, but from presence.
This book is for you.

Start Here...

Scan the QR code below to access free regulation tools to support your journey and explore ways we can stay connected. Whether you're looking for practical resources or deeper support, I'd love to walk alongside you as you step into regulated, purpose-driven leadership.

You don't have to figure it all out alone—let's begin together.

REGULATE TO
RISE

THE HIDDEN KEY
TO POWERFUL LEADERSHIP
AND PERSONAL PEACE

SAM WILLING

Praise for *Regulate to Rise*

"*Regulate to Rise* isn't just a book—it's an extension of Sam Willing's powerful executive coaching practice. Every chapter feels like a conversation that reconnects you to why you wanted to be a leader in the first place. With clear advice and practical tips, this book will help you learn to shift from reaction to response and from urgency or 'hustle' to curiosity. I'm deeply grateful for Sam's influence on my life and leadership, and I can't recommend this book highly enough to anyone seeking a real and sustainable transformation to becoming a more authentic, grounded, and peaceful leader."

— Dr. Nancy Whiting, CEO Recludix Pharma

"*Regulate to Rise* gave me language and a repeatable framework for leading well when it's hardest. Sam's reminder that 'Joy is not the same as happiness' clarified why chasing quick wins never steadies a team—and her question, 'How do we lean into joy in the midst of suffering?' is answered with practical tools that hold up in real pressure. She shows that regulated, values-aligned leadership isn't soft; it's the discipline that makes decisions wiser, cultures more human, and innovation more consistent. I recognized my own path in her framing of resilience—not avoiding emotion, but learning to 'ride the wave' with the confidence you'll return to strong functioning—and I've used her pause-and-recalibrate approach to navigate tough seasons while showing up better for my family, my colleagues, and the people who rely on me. This book met me where I am and called me forward to lead with steadiness, authenticity, and connection."

— Omar Shahine, Corporate Vice President, Microsoft

"*Regulate to Rise* is a gift to anyone feeling the weight of leadership or simply the pace of modern life. Sam Willing bridges science and soul with practical tools that bring peace, presence, and authentic power. Her message aligns with the heart of my own work in *The Truth Within the Lie*: When we slow down and meet ourselves with honesty and compassion, we discover the freedom to lead and live from truth, not tension. This book is grounding, liberating, and for all of us, not just executives."

— Dana Grant, International Life Coach, Speaker and Bestselling Author of *The Truth Within the Lie*

"*Regulate to Rise* bridges the gap between inner regulation and organizational results. Sam Willing names what most leadership books overlook—the nervous system is the hidden driver of trust, decision quality, and cultural stability. Her work equips leaders not just to manage pressure but to transform how their teams perform and grow."

— Paul Harstrom, Founder & CEO, LEAD Diligently

"In an age where AI is transforming how we work, *Regulate to Rise* is a powerful reminder of what will always set great leaders apart—presence, compassion, and self-awareness. Sam Willing offers a deeply human and practical guide for leaders navigating constant change, bridging the worlds of technology and humanity with clarity and care.

What stands out:

- Human + AI Partnership: While AI enhances productivity, this book highlights that human regulation, empathy, and discernment are what make technology meaningful and responsible.

- Modern Leadership in a Digital World: As leaders guide hybrid teams and drive digital transformation, nervous system regulation becomes essential for making wise, ethical, and creative decisions. Sam's insights offer tools not just for performance, but for sustainable leadership.

- Grounded in Experience: With 25+ years in corporate HR, Sam distills hard-earned lessons into a framework that's both honest and actionable. Her message resonates with leaders who want to lead with more presence, not just pressure.

- Aligned with Growth Mindset and Purpose-Driven Culture: The book complements Microsoft's commitment to empowering people and fostering environments where innovation and well-being coexist.

This is more than a leadership book—it's a call to shift from reactive to regulated leadership. Sam shows that when leaders learn to regulate their inner world, everything changes in the outer one."

— Seth Patton, General Manager, Microsoft 365 Copilot,
Product Marketing

Foreword

Regulate to Rise is an invitation to step into something essential, something we've needed all along but perhaps haven't had the courage or the tools to fully pursue.

For years, my own focus has been on helping leaders live and lead with greater intentionality, especially when it comes to their development and their efforts to build trust. At a time when distrust has become the default in too many places, and when leaders are often stretched to the breaking point, the call to move from reactivity to intentionality has never been more urgent. Trust within us, trust between us, and trust around us all depend on leaders who are willing to do the deeper inner work.

Sam Willing is such a leader, and this book is her courageous offering.

Sam is not only a personal friend but also a trusted colleague. I've had the privilege of watching her invest in leaders with honesty, vulnerability, and skill. She is one of those rare people who can hold both depth and approachability at the same time. In *Regulate to Rise,* she does just that: she takes us deep into the essential practice of self-regulation while keeping the pathway clear, practical, and human.

This book matters because emotional regulation matters. It matters for our personal peace. It matters for the trust others place in us. And it matters for the resilience our organizations so desperately need. Sam names what many of us know but often avoid: the way we handle our inner world, our triggers, emotions, and reactions, shapes the kind of leaders we become and the kind of cultures we create.

What strikes me about Sam's writing is her willingness to tell the truth. She doesn't pretend to have it all figured out, nor does she shy away from the realities of harm, tension, and paradox. She shares her own story not as a polished model of perfection, but as a living example of courage, wholeness, and healing in process. In doing so, she gives us permission to tell the truth about our own lives and leadership.

As I read, I was reminded of the leaders I've seen in both the trenches of pressure and the opportunities of growth. Those who learn to regulate not only rise themselves, they help those around them rise as well. They create teams where trust can grow, where people feel safe enough to contribute, and where organizations can move from fragmented reactions to intentional impact.

This is not simply a leadership manual. It is a mirror and a map. A mirror that reflects the truth of our humanity, our strengths, our struggles, our need for healing. And a map that points us toward something more whole, more resilient, and more trustworthy.

Sam's gift in these pages is to weave together vulnerability and wisdom, story and science, personal narrative and practical tools. She extends a conversation I felt called to begin when I wrote *Composed: The Heart and Science of Leading Under Pressure* and created the *Leading Under Pressure Inventory*. She calls us not only to composure under pressure and to intentionality, but to a new presence in our daily lives, to purpose, to peace, and to a new way of being.

If you are a leader, and I believe every one of us is in some way, this book will challenge you. It will stretch you. It will also comfort you, reminding you that you are not alone in the tensions you feel. Most of all, it will invite you into the kind of wholeness that sustains trust in real time, in real relationships, and in the real challenges you face.

I am grateful to call Sam a friend and a fellow traveler. She is brave enough to write the kind of book that not only informs but transforms. My hope is that as you read *Regulate to Rise,* you will find yourself invited into that transformation too.

So I encourage you, don't just skim these pages. Let them work on you. Let them unsettle you in the best of ways. Let them invite you to the deeper work of becoming a regulated and resilient leader, one who is trustworthy, present, and intentional. When leaders rise in this way, the people they serve rise too. And that is how real change begins.

—Dr. Rob McKenna
Founder & CEO, WiLD Leaders, Inc.
Author of *Whole Leaders, Wild Trust: The Courageous Path to Personal, Relational, and Organizational Change*

Table of Contents

Introduction 1

Chapter 1: Integrating Thinking, Feeling, and Doing in Leadership 5

Chapter 2: What Is Regulation, And Why Does It Matter? 15

Chapter 3: The Ripple Effect of Leaders and Their Nervous Systems 27

Chapter 4: What Triggers Us Into Dysregulation 37

Chapter 5: How Regulation Forms Company Culture 55

Chapter 6: The Role of Compassion and Self-Compassion 65

Chapter 7: How Regulation Builds Resilience 75

Chapter 8: Leading and Identity 87

Chapter 9: Integration and Alignment 97

Conclusion 117

Acknowledgements 121

Citations and Resources 123

Introduction

WHAT IF THE DIFFERENCE between thriving in leadership and just surviving in leadership isn't skill or strategy; it's nervous system regulation? Grounded in both science and story, this book shows how regulated leaders create meaningful, lasting impact from the inside out, without losing themselves or what matters most along the way.

For as long as I can remember, I have been interested in growth and development. From an early age, I was given opportunities to lead. I developed a strong ability to connect deeply with others and offer guidance and wisdom that, in retrospect, was beyond my years. I was often called an old soul. I took great pleasure in helping others and solving problems. In college, my nickname was "counselor," and I took that role on with pride. It is no wonder that I ended up choosing human resources as my career path and have spent the last twenty-nine years guiding, mediating, and problem-solving for leaders across many companies and many functions.

I have experienced, borne witness to, and cleaned up just about every employee relations issue out there and have been part of guiding companies through high-pressure, pivotal moments such as acquisitions, startups, and sadly, failure. Needless to say, I have observed a wide range of leadership behaviors: the good, the neutral, and the dysfunctional. In fact, I used to joke that someday I would write a book called *Tales from a Corporate Clean-Up Girl* and share all of my experiences "cleaning up" after ill-equipped leaders, because often I found myself exhausted by and disappointed in the leaders

I worked with. I was disappointed in the inconsistency, dysfunction, and damaging behaviors they displayed, particularly under pressure.

A couple of years ago, I had a life-changing experience that led me down a different path. I lost my mom to breast cancer. The loss and grief I experienced and still process today changed me forever. It called into question life, its temporary nature, priorities, my self-care, and presence. I chose to embark on a healing journey. I wanted to know myself better, sort through some of the patterns and ways I limited myself, and make choices and set priorities differently. I wanted freedom over fear and wholeness over fragmentation. As I did the work, much of it centered around healing and regulating my nervous system, I noticed something. I was showing up differently. My ability to handle pressure was different. I was calmer, more confident, and knocked off course less easily. I also noticed that I wasn't taking things on and gripping to outcomes like I had in the past, always trying to control and save. I was responding instead of reacting: I was different, I was regulated, and my work was thriving.

As I paid attention to this difference and became more and more aware of the dysregulation of the leaders around me and the ways it negatively impacted business, people, and culture, an idea started to emerge. What if nervous system regulation and effective leadership were linked? What difference would it make if leaders knew how to regulate themselves and operate in a calm, practical way that was rooted in their core values? I have come to believe that a leader's ability to regulate themselves is the key to effective leadership, which is not only crucial for building a successful company where business and people thrive but also for leading whole lives effectively and authentically with clarity, confidence, and consistency.

As I reflect on my HR work over the last twenty-nine years, through all the issues I have been part of cleaning up, all the drama and tumult, at its root was a dysregulated leader bumping up against other dysregulated human beings in a significantly dysregulated world.

There were many times in my HR journey when I threatened to leave the function, tired of working so hard to drive positive change and improve leadership behavior, only to realize that there seemed to be a perpetual cycle. In most cases, while leaders could change their behaviors at a baseline and prescriptive level, the changes didn't stick, particularly in times of pressure. I found it incredibly frustrating, and found myself judging the leaders I was working with and for, until now. Until I fully understood the concept of dysregulation and drew the link between regulation and leadership.

Now, I look back and can hold space with compassion for those leaders; they were human beings, placed in high-pressure leadership roles with little to no training in leadership or regulation. Most of them had spent their lives pushing, forcing, and striving. Many had no idea what their core values were. And yet, inside, they were struggling with their own human experience. They lived and led disconnected, their identities rooted in their title, role, and power, and they were not whole leaders, which made it impossible for them to hold vision, inspire others, and execute business strategies where people and business thrived.

One of the things I learned through my mom's sickness and death was that as human beings, we can hold differing and sometimes opposite emotions, feelings, and views at the same time. For example, I realized that I could hold deep grief and yet experience deep joy. So, while I am telling you of my compassion for such leaders, I want you to know that I also hold conviction for them. The truth is that while they navigate their own human experience and need compassion, healing, and grounding, their actions, decisions, and behaviors directly impact those around them. They are paid high salaries to navigate times of pressure and reap the rewards. They are trusted to run companies and make decisions. They are counted on. So, while this is not a call out, it is a call up: a call to know better and then do better, a call to operate with a great deal of curiosity, humility, and courage.

I've always believed that one of my most important roles as an HR leader is to actively seek ways to alleviate the anxiety of work, so that humans can focus and do their best work without excessive drama and distraction. In my coaching work, I believe one of my most important roles is to help leaders achieve a deep level of self-awareness regarding their impact on others and themselves, while maintaining a balance of truth and grace.

As I have integrated regulatory work into my coaching, I am witnessing profound transformation and a refreshed energy in my clients. I help leaders and organizations move from burnout and breakdown to clarity, confidence, and sustainable impact. Because when a leader learns to regulate, everything changes, from decision-making and team dynamics to trust, resilience, and results. This is more than theory. It's practice. It's transformation. It's the hidden key to powerful leadership and personal peace.

Pairing regulation work with leadership work allows them to walk in their true identities as leaders, deeply rooted in their core values, driving impact and finding success, all without sacrificing their most important priorities, including themselves. I have seen leaders move from a fear of failure to a confidence in knowing who they are and why they are here, understanding that their value lies in their *being*, not in their *doing,* and success should be measured by impact, not just outcomes.

In our performance-based society, that is freedom. I have seen cultures change and teams grow as leaders bring clarity and confidence to their vision and align their people strategy with their business strategy. In this book, I share stories of my own experiences, as well as those of others, plus guidance and resources on where to start. Whether you're an executive seeking personal transformation, a founder navigating complexity, or a company committed to building a more human, high-performing culture, this work is for you.

As you read this, I encourage you to stay open and in doing so, reflect and analyze your life, your leadership, and your impact on others. Be curious, courageous, and always have a great deal of self-compassion. The world needs you: all of you, the whole you, the regulated you.

CHAPTER 1

Integrating Thinking, Feeling, and Doing in Leadership

ONE OF THE MOST OVERLOOKED aspects of effective leadership is the internal tension many leaders feel between thinking and feeling. In high-stakes environments, especially in industries like biotech, where failure is frequent and pressure is high, leaders often default to one or the other: they either lean into logic and decisiveness or immerse themselves in empathy and relational connection. But the truth is, sustainable leadership (regulated leadership) requires both.

On October 1, 2024, I ended my twenty-nine-year career in corporate human resources. The company I was with at the time, a small public biotech company, failed its final clinical trial. While I always knew failure was an option, it was heartbreaking for the team members who had spent years developing a drug that would have been groundbreaking for Alzheimer's patients and their families. As the failure sank in, so did the reality that it was now my job to plan and orchestrate the mass layoff of seventy percent of employees, which would also include myself and several executives. I was presented with both opportunity and choice: an opportunity to assist the company in executing a business strategy that would, hopefully, lead to the company continuing on in some capacity, and the choice to exercise compassion and care for others in the process.

While it was incredibly difficult, I had a deep knowing that I was the perfect person for the job and put my energy and effort into planning and executing a layoff that was transparent, honest, and provided as much support as possible. I worked on messaging and special touches that allowed everyone to feel the impact of the loss while expressing gratitude and appreciating each other. We had an open day where we brought in food and invited those impacted to come in, hang out, and say goodbye as they packed up their belongings. Some couldn't bear to come; the ones that came shared laughter and tears. I remember sitting outside the building in my car every morning for the weeks leading up to the layoff, holding an imperfect wooden heart in my hand (my favorite touchpoint) and praying that I would be used as a light as I entered the building, that anyone who interacted with me would feel cared for and seen.

So often in business, we spend so much energy on beginnings and excitement, and then rush through pain and hardship, just wanting the pain to be over. More often than not, we are uncomfortable with suffering, whether that of our own or that of others. But when we rush, we miss opportunities to impact those around us and extend compassion in the midst of suffering, discounting the need for humanity. We disconnect our head, heart, and hands in the very moments where those connections matter the most. It takes a deep connection to our values and intentional effort to be present, authentic, and compassionate.

Illustration by Ali Willing

Operating from our head involves intellect, strategy, and decision-making; operating from our heart involves values, empathy, and emotional intelligence; and operating from our hands involves execution, action, and follow-through. In business, we have largely been taught that operating from our heart is a weakness, so we compartmentalize and work hard to operate from our head: objective truth and facts. But finding the balance between head and heart is where the most authentic and successful leadership lives, where our best thinking and problem-solving come into play. If we only operate solely from our heads, it is easy for us to make decisions that have a negative impact on people; if we operate solely from our hearts, it is easy for us to make decisions that have a negative impact on the business; and if we operate solely from our hands, it is easy for us to make real messes as we keep busy *doing*, without the strategy of the head or the empathy of the heart.

It is highly likely that over the course of your career, you have taken one of the mainstream personality tests: Myers-Briggs, Predictive Index, DISC, StrengthsFinder. I have taken most of them, and the results are always similar in that I am a heart-driven person, high in empathy and compassion. As I reached the executive level in my career, I was always an outlier, the heart person, the feeler, the people-person at the executive table. There were times I felt so out of place, like I didn't belong, until I realized my heart was exactly what these executive teams needed. My ability to balance my compassionate heart with intellect was what made me a great HR and culture leader.

In Dr. Rob McKenna's book *Composed*, his research sheds important light on this very dynamic. His work reveals that those who tend to be less empathetic and more head-driven often display stronger moment-to-moment self-regulation and are less likely to interpret challenges as personal attacks, allowing them to remain grounded and make decisions from a place of objectivity. In our society, these individuals are often promoted for their perceived clarity, control, and ability to produce results. On the other hand, those higher in empathy excel at connecting to others, understanding systemic impact, and sensing the emotional undercurrents in a room, yet they may struggle with emotional overwhelm, especially when they absorb the stress and emotions of others as their own.

> **WITHOUT EMOTIONAL CONNECTIVE TISSUE, OUR WORLD BECOMES RUN BY THE COMPULSIONS OF INDIVIDUAL LEADERS WHO LACK THE NATURAL ABILITY TO TAKE IN NEW INFORMATION, INTEGRATE FEEDBACK FROM OTHERS, AND CONNECT WITH THE DEEPER EMOTIONAL NEEDS OF THOSE AROUND THEM.**
>
> **— DR. ROB MCKENNA**

This is something I can relate to all too well. I have had to learn over the years how not to take on others' emotions. I have had to fire far too many people in my career. In fact, I once had a CEO tell me that I was "really good at firing people," not exactly the legacy an empathetic and compassionate person wants to leave. What no one knew was that while I mastered the art of hard conversations and terminations and could handle them with a balance of compassion and firmness, once the conversation was over, I went to the bathroom or got in my car and cried. I wasn't crying because it was the wrong thing to do, but because of the impact on another human being's life. It hurt my heart.

Dr. McKenna discusses letting go of the old labels of "thinker" or "feeler" and instead recognizing that the most powerful leaders are not one or the other, but both: thinkers who feel and feelers who think. Regulated leaders recognize the strength in each tendency and work to bring them into alignment. They slow down, create space to regulate their internal responses, and then choose their next action not just from intellect or emotion, but from an integration of the two. This is where the work of head, heart, and hands comes to life.

This balanced approach, when practiced consistently, results in authentic leadership. After many years of being around leaders and leading myself, I know that people follow authenticity. As a leader, you may be responsible for casting vision and inspiration, at times, seeing a vision that others don't. I have worked with many CEOs; every single one of them was accused at times of being toxically optimistic, and at a certain point, I realized that this must be a requirement of the CEO role. Yet the difference between the CEOs that people followed and the CEOs that people resisted was their level of authenticity.

A few years ago, I delivered 360-degree feedback to a CEO I was coaching. 360s are an approach to gathering feedback from multiple colleagues in order to gain a complete (360-degree view) of a leader's impact. This CEO wanted to be a great leader; he was charismatic, energetic, and had worked hard to establish himself as a "values-based" leader, building a "values-based" company. As I reviewed the feedback, it became clear that there was a disconnect between how he desired to show up and the impact he desired to have on others, and what was actually happening. It was reported that his behavior under pressure often went against the values on the wall. When he was under pressure, he became aggressive, didn't filter his words or actions carefully, and treated others poorly. The feedback also reported that he was detached from employees and didn't give authentic recognition when employees went above and beyond. He was taken aback by the feedback; after all, he had put significant effort into the culture at his company.

We talked about the fact that employees can handle a lot, but what they can't handle is hypocrisy. His behaviors that conflicted with the values did real damage to morale. As he processed, we set some goals around what he was committed to working on. He chose recognition as one of his focus areas. A couple of weeks later, we met, and he proudly communicated that he was doing amazing in his efforts around recognition. He told me that he had printed out a list of every employee, and he went down the list and sent each person a shout-out for their work through the internal, public software recognition system the company used, but I cautioned him about making sure his approach was authentic and intentional and not part of a box-checking exercise.

Sure enough, a couple of weeks later, an employee commented to the HR team that employees were aware of what the CEO was doing; they could see every shout-out on the big screen around the office, most of them generic and obviously alphabetical. The lesson? Inauthentic action, even if it seems well-intended, can do more damage than doing nothing at all.

His approach backfired, creating more distrust and confirmation that he was detached, and perpetuating the perception that he didn't care. Though I can't judge whether or not he cared, I will admit that he did put a lot of effort into trying to build the culture. But in the end, he was using his head and his hands, sometimes just his hands, and his actions were void of the heart, which had a negative compounding effect on the culture. If he had slowed down, integrated his heart, and asked himself the right questions, it could have been so different.

So, how do we balance the three energy centers? The first thing it requires is slowing down and being present. If you are a high-performing individual growing your career, you have probably heard advice about being present, yet it's easier said than done. We keep a pace that is unsustainable in many ways, and yet, we sustain it. We sustain it, but we make many sacrifices in the sustaining, many times sacrificing ourselves and our own well-being. Even with our best intentions, the world is working against us. We bounce from one distraction to another, from smartphones to watches. Our time is never off limits, it seems, and we've convinced ourselves that we can effectively multitask not only in our actions but also in our listening.

The truth is, when we try to focus on multiple things, it pulls us out of being present or doing anything well. A 2019 MIT Sloan Management Review article titled "The Impossibility of Focusing on Two Things at Once" states that our brains aren't designed to focus on more than one thing at a time, and attempting to do so can impair our ability to concentrate, leading to decreased performance and increased stress. It makes it feel impossible to slow down, get quiet, and focus. Many of my clients express feeling guilty for slowing down or turning on "Do Not Disturb." Their phones are the first thing they grab in the morning and the last thing they look at at night. They eat family dinners with their phones, and if they don't have their phones, they feel relieved to have their watch to notify them of anything "urgent." Some of them have even admitted to bringing their phones into yoga or church. Sometimes, it feels like nothing is sacred anymore.

The reality is, we tend to demonize rest, even when we know we need it. We treat rest as an inconvenient intruder, which makes it difficult, albeit impossible, to stay grounded and regulated. Over time, we train our brains to operate in an elevated state of hyperawareness all the time, and we place our value in being accessible.

Our constant accessibility feeds our anxiety and makes it challenging to make balanced decisions from all three centers: our head, heart, and hands, to stay out of a reactive state and take what I call productive action.

Most leaders I work with are action takers. It is rare that a leader comes to me for coaching in speeding up. Most of the time, it's for slowing down, prioritizing, doing less, and practicing presence. They have a propensity for action; action is familiar to them. Action got them to where they are, and they believe that sustaining that success requires more of it. But often, so much of their action is fueled by anxiety and fear, leading them to take "quick action," or reaction, that lacks deliberate intention and self-awareness. When we take action from this dysregulated state, it can create unnecessary churn and drama, which harms the business by distracting from the work at hand.

Remember the CEO above? His quick action was a reaction to the negative feedback he received in his 360, which resulted in negative churn in the organization. I want you to think of action from a place of intention. Pause and ask yourself: *Given my desired outcome, what is the most productive action I can take?* To do that, you must be able to move out of a place of reaction and into a place of productive response and action. This is what regulation is all about.

There is so much power in a pause. When you slow down and create space to reflect, you unlock the ability to ask questions that lead to wiser, more human-centered decisions. Instead of rushing to fix or control, you explore possibilities with intention, weigh the ripple effects of your actions on others, and seek wisdom from trusted voices: a coach, a mentor, an HR partner, or other people close to the work who hold clear insights. From there, you don't just build a strategy; you build a head- and heart-aligned strategy. And when you move forward with that alignment, your actions become more purposeful, your communication more grounded, and your leadership more stabilizing. You'll feel the shift, not just in yourself, but in your team. When you regulate yourself, you regulate the room. Less reactivity *in* you means less reactivity *around* you. That is how real influence begins.

One of the most important keys to being able to connect your head, heart, and hands, besides tangible experience, knowledge, and skills, is understanding the importance of who you are beyond what you do. What are your core values? What is your identity rooted in? We will talk about core values and identity throughout the book, but to do so, we must first define them.

"Core values" are deeply held beliefs and principles that shape how you think, make decisions, and interact with others. You can think of them as a compass that informs your purpose, integrity, and alignment. Put simply, they define how you show up in all aspects of your life, including your role as a leader. When leaders are clear on their core values, they tend to show up with consistent actions and behaviors and an authentic presence, and others have an easier time making the choice to follow them. Their core values are not treated as negotiable depending on stress level or pressure, but reflect the core of who they are, day in and day out.

"Identity," on the other hand, is an internal sense of who you are that is made up of experiences, beliefs, motivations, and self-perceptions: how you see yourself, what you stand for, and how you show up in the world.

Core values are foundational to identity. They serve as an anchor to help stabilize you. When your core values and identity are in alignment, you show up with more confidence, clarity, resilience, and authenticity. When they are not, you experience burnout, internal conflict, and anxiety.

One of the most common issues I discover with leaders is that they don't pause to identify what their core values are or what their identity is rooted in. Many of them report that they are values-driven leaders but struggle to specify what those values are and how their actions and behaviors reflect those values. They have built their identity around external factors like their job title or status. But some of the biggest transformations I have witnessed have been leaders doing the work around identifying their core values, defining their true identity, and identifying strategies to live those things out.

At the heart of regulated leadership is the courage to slow down, to ask better questions, and to lead with deep intentionality. It's about integrating the intellect of your head, the compassion in your heart, and the purpose in your action in a way that honors both the business and the people in it. It's about insight meeting empathy, and strategy meeting soul. The leader who can pause, reflect, empathize, and then act with clarity and compassion is the one who fosters trust, diffuses reactivity, and builds cultures capable of withstanding pressure. We don't need more leaders who avoid their hearts in the name of performance or lose clarity in the name of compassion. We need leaders who know how to connect, discern, and respond, leaders who are whole.

As you move forward in this book, I invite you to approach your own leadership with curiosity, humility, and honesty. Start noticing your patterns. Ask yourself not just *what you're doing* but *who you're becoming*. And remember: the goal isn't perfection, but presence. When you learn to lead from a place of self-awareness, aligned values, and productive regulation, you'll not only create more impact, you'll become the kind of leader people trust, follow, and remember.

Reader Action:

1. When you think of your current leadership style, which of the three centers do you use the most, and which do you use the least? Take a moment to journal about one recent leadership moment where you noticed this pattern show up. What might it have looked like if you approached it from a more integrated place?

2. Set aside five minutes each day this week for an intentional "leadership pause" before a key meeting or interaction. Breathe and ask yourself these questions:

   - *What am I thinking?*
   - *What am I feeling?*
   - *What is my desired outcome?*
   - *What does it look like for me to show up integrated?*

CHAPTER 2

What Is Regulation, And Why Does It Matter?

NERVOUS SYSTEM REGULATION has become a buzzword. Therapists, doctors, coaches, influencers; everyone's talking about it. And for good reason. Our nervous systems play a massive role in how we experience stress, how we respond under pressure, and how we recover. But my journey into regulation didn't start because I wanted to study it or was even interested in it. It started because a few years ago, I found myself in crisis.

At forty-seven years old, I went to therapy for the first time, not because I wanted to explore nervous system science or optimize my performance, but because my mom was dying of breast cancer, my stress levels were through the roof, and I was barely holding it together. At the time, I was leading HR at a high-growth biotech startup that had started to struggle, navigating the transition into empty-nesting with my last child heading off to college, and caregiving for my mom.

I knew I was heading toward burnout. I could feel it. But instead of slowing down, I did what high performers often do: I pushed harder. I doubled down. I told myself I could outrun the pain, that I wasn't going to give up, that I'd always been the one who could keep it together. But what I've learned about resistance is that what we resist persists. When we are living out of alignment, life has a way of squeezing us. And I was getting squeezed.

The pressure started showing up in my body. I developed a persistent eye twitch that spread down my face. I broke out in hives. I stopped sleeping. I started taking sleeping pills. Wine became a nightly routine. I took anti-anxiety medication. I shopped more than usual, all of it an attempt to soothe something inside me I couldn't quite name. In a particularly ironic moment, I even let an esthetician inject Botox into my eyelid to stop the twitching. It sounds absurd now, but at the time, I was willing to do almost anything to keep functioning.

And then came the moment that broke the illusion.

I was in a tense executive Zoom meeting, one of those awful, high-stakes, no-traction meetings where everyone's dysregulation shows up loud and clear. I was frustrated as I had been watching the culture I cared so deeply about and helped build get damaged on a daily basis as the company struggled. In a moment of desperation, I picked up my phone and texted my husband: *"Ugh, I need a new job..."*

Except I sent it to my CEO.

Let that sink in. This high-performing, executive-level perfectionist accidentally sent the text to her boss. Seconds later, when he responded, *"We should talk?"* I knew I had a choice. I could play it off, blame the meeting, turn it into a poorly timed, sarcastic joke. But something in me was done hiding. So I owned it. I texted back: *"Yes. That was meant for my husband, but I think it was divine intervention that it went to you. Let's talk."*

Now, keep in mind that we were still on Zoom with all of our colleagues as this happened. I was mortified. After the call, I burst into tears; I was humiliated. My husband hugged me as I sobbed, and I felt his shoulders gently start shaking. He was laughing.

"It's not funny!" I said, "I don't make mistakes like that."

He smiled and said, "Exactly. That's why it's funny. It's like God finally got tired of waiting for you."

The next day, I resigned. The CEO was so gracious, offering me a leave of absence, part-time, or a consulting role, but by that point, I was so physically uncomfortable, I knew I had to leave.

When I left the company I helped build, I grieved hard. I cried over the job, the title, the security. But mostly, I cried because I realized how much of my identity was wrapped up in proving my worth. How had I drifted so far from what really matters?

I told myself I'd take a month off to recover, then dive into my next thing. But life had other plans. That one month turned into nine. And in that space, I experienced some of the hardest and most beautiful days of my life. I was fully present for my mom's last nine months. I slowed down. I started therapy. I journaled. I moved my body gently. I let myself grieve, and create, and breathe.

I didn't know it at the time, but I was learning to regulate.

It was uncomfortable. There were days I wondered if I'd ever return to work. But I knew I was being protected. That sacred slowness was teaching me how to feel calm in my body, really calm, not the performative kind I'd faked for years. During this time, I also learned that we can hold conflicting emotions. I felt grief and joy, sadness and gratitude, love and loss, all at once. And I began, slowly, to surrender…for the most part.

I say "for the most part" because two days before my mom died, I accepted a new corporate role, as the Chief People Officer at a biotech in crisis. A decision I definitely didn't have the emotional reserves to make. But alas, in my effort to control something amidst life's uncontrollable circumstances, I said yes. That job was in the most stressful environment I had ever been in; the cultural and people issues were intense, but I was different. Grief and healing had changed me. I felt rooted, regulated, and focused on the impact I could make in others' lives. Of course, there were times I slipped into dysregulation, but I had new tools to bring myself back quickly. And that made all the difference.

So why does regulation matter? Because leadership under pressure is inevitable. Life under pressure is inevitable. But living in a constant state of dysregulation? That's optional. Regulation is the foundation. It's the thing that helps you return to yourself again and again, no matter how intense the moment. It's not about being calm all the time. It's about knowing how to come back.

Let's talk about what regulation really means and why it's the key to sustainable leadership, impact, and a life that actually feels like yours.

"Nervous system regulation" is a term used to describe the body's ability to adapt to pressure and stress. It utilizes both the sympathetic and parasympathetic nervous systems. The sympathetic nervous system is our fight-or-flight response, and the parasympathetic nervous system is our rest-and-digest response. Our body is constantly toggling between the two, and when we are regulated, we are able to transition smoothly between them.

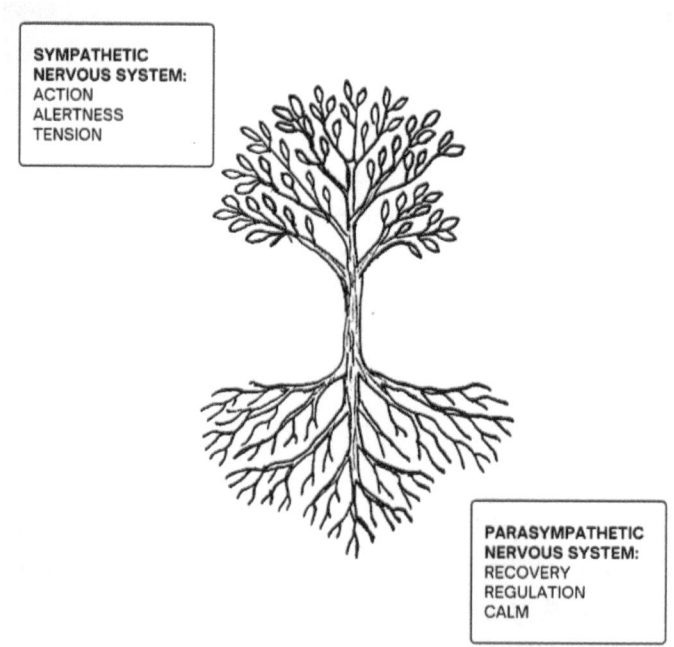

Illustration by Ali Willing

There are many functions of the nervous system in the body. I am not a doctor or a scientist, but here is a simple list for reference:

- To send and receive messages and transmit signals between the brain, spinal cord, and the rest of the body.

- To control body movements and direct both voluntary (e.g., walking) and involuntary (e.g., breathing) muscle actions.

- To process sensory information and interpret data from the senses.

- To regulate internal functions and maintain body functions like heart rate, digestion, and temperature.

- To support learning and memory and enable thinking, decision-making, memory storage, and emotional response.

- To manage stress, calm, and balance sympathetic and parasympathetic responses.

- To coordinate reflexes and quickly respond to danger without needing to think (e.g., pulling your hand away from something hot).

Your nervous system is made up of two main parts and spans your entire body, from head to toe.

1. The central nervous system consists of the brain and spinal cord. The brain serves as the command center, processing information and controlling thoughts, emotions, and decisions. The spinal cord connects the brain to the rest of the body, carrying messages to and from it.

2. The peripheral nervous system is made up of nerves that branch out from the spinal cord and extend throughout the body, including the limbs, organs, and skin. These nerves relay signals between the body and the central nervous system, enabling sensory

input and motor responses. The autonomic nervous system, a subdivision of the peripheral nervous system, regulates involuntary functions such as heart rate, breathing, digestion, and body temperature, and includes the sympathetic and parasympathetic systems, which help maintain balance in the body's internal environment.

Before we go deeper, I must first explain the difference between nervous system regulation and emotional regulation.

"Nervous system regulation" is the process of calming your autonomic nervous system to return to a calm and grounded state. It involves your heart rate, breathing, muscle tension, and energy levels. The goal is to restore physiological balance so your body feels calm and safe, and able to maintain a responsive state versus a reactive one. "Emotional regulation" is your ability to control your emotional responses, especially in triggering or emotional events. Emotional regulation involves things like naming your emotions, choosing your response, and expressing it in a healthy way, in a state of self-awareness and reflection. The goal is to maintain psychological balance and respond to emotions with intention and resilience.

Emotional regulation depends on nervous system regulation. When your nervous system is dysregulated, it is more difficult for your brain to access the parts of the brain that support emotional control. Nervous system regulation is the pathway to emotional regulation.

This is why, when I coach leaders, I always say: Mindset work alone is not enough. You can journal your intentions, recite affirmations, and develop all the mental strategies in the world, but if your nervous system is in a constant state of survival, the work won't stick. We've put so much emphasis on mindset in the personal growth and leadership world, and while important, if your body has been trained to stay on high alert, and your nervous system doesn't know what safety and calm actually feel like, then your brain will have a hard time accessing that mindset work when it matters most.

That's why leaders sometimes feel frustrated or defeated by the very tools that were meant to help. They've done the work, they know the language, and they can say all the "right" things, but in moments of real pressure or anxiety, the tools fall flat. Not because the tools are wrong, but because the system that's trying to use them is still in survival mode. To lead effectively under pressure, you have to retrain your brain and body to recognize what it feels like to be regulated, calm, grounded, and safe. Only then can you truly absorb new strategies, make clear decisions, and respond instead of react. Regulation isn't a nice-to-have; it's the foundation for sustainable leadership growth.

Now, let's talk about the autonomic nervous system, composed of the sympathetic and parasympathetic nervous systems.

The sympathetic nervous system is the branch of the nervous system that activates the fight, flight, or freeze response during stressful or dangerous situations and prepares the body to take action. Think of it as your body's emergency response system. When activated, you might experience increased heart rate, faster breathing, and a heightened sense of alertness in your muscles. It also slows down digestion and releases cortisol, adrenaline, and noradrenaline into the body.

The parasympathetic nervous system is the branch of the nervous system responsible for the rest-and-digest state and helps the body recover, restore, and return to balance after stress. Think of your parasympathetic nervous system as your body's recovery and regulation system. When activated, you might experience a slower heart rate, deeper breathing, and a general sense of relaxation. It also stimulates digestion and supports healing and immunity. The chemicals released during the activation of this state include serotonin, oxytocin, and acetylcholine.

We need both systems. One protects us and gets us ready for action, while the other allows us to perform in a calm and relaxed state. In a perfect world, these two systems work seamlessly together, and you are able to flow back and forth between them as needed. But because we live in a highly dysregulated world constantly pulling on us for attention and fast reactions, the default for many of us has become reacting instead of responding to pressure. When we operate in fight, flight, or freeze mode with our sympathetic nervous system activated, it creates tension and tightness in the body, which, when sustained over time, becomes our new normal, causing the brain to reset its baseline, forget what true calm feels like, and accept our reactive behaviors as simply "the way the world is."

As leaders, the pressure, tension, and tightness we experience in daily interactions and decisions can often push us into reacting emotionally, rather than responding with calmness and the clarity needed to separate our emotions from the task or decision at hand. Not only can functioning too often in your sympathetic nervous system damage your relationships, your reputation, or your business, but there are also significant health impacts associated with the chemicals involved.

Activation of the sympathetic nervous system releases cortisol, adrenaline, and noradrenaline. Cortisol helps sustain alertness over time by increasing blood sugar, suppressing non-essential functions like digestion and immune response, and providing long-term energy, while adrenaline and noradrenaline prepare you for action. On the other hand, activation of the parasympathetic nervous system releases serotonin, oxytocin, and acetylcholine, chemicals of relaxation and recovery. When we are in this state, we have an easier time operating from a calm state and connecting with others.

The idea is not that you never want to activate your sympathetic nervous system; sometimes it is helpful, like before you deliver a speech or compete in a sporting event. The key is to be able to identify when you are in an activated state and bring yourself back down to a regulated state quickly.

Imagine being a firefighter, eating dinner, and watching sports with your colleagues. Everyone is relaxed, telling jokes, laughing, and then suddenly, the alarm goes off. There is a fire. The energy of everyone at the station changes quickly, as adrenaline and noradrenaline pump through their bodies, fueling them for action. As you approach the fire, cortisol kicks in, enabling you to fight it at a sustained pace with enough energy while reserving what you can in case the fire drags on.

These chemicals are necessary in short-term bursts, but if the firefighters stay in this state for too long, they will start to break down. They will be physically, mentally, and emotionally exhausted. It is in this state that we see relationships crack, decision-making suffer, and burnout ensue.

The firefighters must be able to return to the station and refuel their minds, bodies, and spirits. And if done well, they will once again be sitting as a team and enjoying each other's company after a brief reprieve.

Sadly, we have normalized living in chronic stress. Anxiety has become the number one issue among American workers, according to a 2024 survey done by Compsych. Our cortisol levels are constantly high, and we medicate ourselves in unhealthy ways like overeating, drinking alcohol, taking prescription medication, or indulging in other vices that hurt us more than help us. Because of this, we break connection with others, isolate ourselves, and allow the stress to take control. As I mentioned in my story, I've been there and kept pushing forward, determined not to lose ground. Little did I realize at the time that I was doing just that, and the ground I was losing was my mental health, well-being, and sense of connection with the people I loved the most.

In my work with clients, one of the first things I do is help them identify when they are slipping into dysregulation and what the triggers and physical symptoms are. The faster they can identify what they are, the faster they can catch themselves and either avoid slipping into dysregulation altogether or bring themselves back to a regulated, calm state more quickly.

When your sympathetic nervous system gets activated and your stress response takes over, you might experience sweating, shallow breathing, dry mouth, a feeling of anxiety in your gut, a flutter in your heart, a tightness in your throat, a buzzing in your head, disrupted sleep, muscle tension, headaches, and the list goes on. These are your warning signals. Your body is getting ready for battle or fleeing a situation that feels unsafe. This is the time you want to be able to draw on your ability to regulate yourself. But if you don't develop and practice regulating when you are *not* in high-pressure moments, you will not be able to regulate when you *are*.

It is all about laying new tracks in your brain and body so that you can identify when you are slipping into a state of dysregulation and trigger your brain with thoughts like, *I'm getting a warning sign, and I know exactly what to do to bring myself back,* before deploying your tools, which we will talk about later.

Nervous system regulation work will be ongoing for the rest of your life. It is not about mastery or perfection. It's about practice. Life is challenging, and while our bodies will continue to instinctively react, how we respond ultimately comes down to practice.

As you become aware of your own dysregulation, you will soon begin to notice the dysregulation of others around you. You will be able to take a step back, observe, and then lead and respond in a different way, a more effective and compassionate way, which will positively impact your team and your organization.

Energy is contagious, and when you choose to uplevel and show up regulated, your meetings, conversations, and high-pressure moments will uplevel too. And the best part is that others experiencing you will rise to meet you as you lead by example.

Reader Action:

1. What are your personal signs of dysregulation, physically, emotionally, and/or behaviorally? Reflect on a recent high-pressure leadership moment. What signals did your body give you? How did you respond? What would a more regulated response look like?

2. Create a pattern map over the next three to five days, making a note each time you feel dysregulated. Ask yourself these questions:

   - *What happened?*
   - *How did it feel in my body?*
   - *What did I do next?*

3. At the end of the week, look for patterns. Are there certain environments, people, or situations that trigger your dysregulation? What does your nervous system tend to do?

CHAPTER 3

The Ripple Effect of Leaders and Their Nervous Systems

PICTURE THIS: You were an HR executive who had recently joined an exciting startup with promising technology. You weren't unhappy in your former HR job, but you were open to a new role if the right one came along, especially one led by a CEO serious about people and culture, where values like integrity, compassion, and resilience weren't just words on a wall, but part of the everyday work. So when a charismatic, well-accomplished CEO offered you the opportunity to join a team that seemed, on the outside, to check all the boxes, you didn't hesitate to say yes.

You felt excitement and anticipation as you were told that your first task would be to establish the company's values. Knowing how foundational values are, you brought in an outside consultant with expertise in the process. Your CEO was supportive. He even stood in front of the company to tout his commitment to culture and emphasize the importance of company values.

The day came when it was time to kick off the values project. The boardroom was filled with the HR team, the C-suite executives, and the level below, consisting of vice presidents and senior directors. The purpose of the meeting was to walk these leaders through the process and the *why* behind it and gain buy-in and support; after all, this was a foundational project for the company.

The CEO entered the meeting late and red-faced, obviously flustered, and took a seat at the head of the boardroom table, his energy altering the room. Something was off. Then, as you introduced the external consultant heading the project, the CEO blurted out, "Why the f%*k are we here?" Everyone startled, and you, panicking, started to explain, reminding him of his prior endorsement. To this, the CEO calmly shook his head and said something to the effect of, "That's right, I forgot about this. Please continue."

The meeting continued with an energy of anxiety and discomfort. The CEO tried to recover by being encouraging and expressing the importance of the project, but the damage was done. Never again would the other leaders of the company believe that the CEO valued culture and company values. Before long, word spread to the staff about the interaction, and an environment of fear, skepticism, and distrust was seeded.

Post-meeting, the CEO voiced his apology for the behavior and admitted that he had walked into the room feeling frustrated and anxious due to an intense conversation with a board member before the meeting. In other words, his behavior had nothing to do with the values project but was simply a reaction to the pressure he had been feeling at that moment. But just like there is no getting the toothpaste back in the tube once it's out... so is the way with moments like this.

This chapter explores the consequences of dysregulation in leadership and the responsibility that comes with power. The ripple effect of a leader's regulation or dysregulation has a profound impact on culture. Leaders operating from a place of stress, reactivity, and unchecked emotion can do permanent damage, while leaders who show up regulated drive innovation, productivity, and positive results in a more sustainable way.

We've all heard the phrase "It starts at the top." We understand what it means, and yet, so often, the top is where the real issues exist. As a leader, you have an opportunity and responsibility to set the tone at your organization. Employees look to you to learn what is expected, tolerated, and rewarded; even the energy you bring into the room has a profound impact. When you carry the energy of frustration, anxiety, or anger, you block connection, progress, and growth.

That said, the pressure and frustration you face are real, and most people can't relate, making being a CEO incredibly lonely. A 2024 survey revealed that twenty-five percent of CEOs reported frequent feelings of loneliness, while an additional fifty-five percent acknowledged experiencing moderate yet significant bouts of loneliness. This sense of isolation is not merely a personal struggle but also has tangible implications for organizational performance, with many CEOs reporting that their loneliness negatively impacts their ability to lead effectively.

When you are at the top, you are held to a higher standard that is reflected through your responsibilities and your paycheck. You are paid the "big bucks" to handle the pressure and prevent it from spilling out onto others. You lose your right to vent, and it can feel impossible to find safe spaces to express fears and insecurities. Research from Korn Ferry shows that CEOs often feel they cannot share openly about uncertainty, fear, or overwhelm, especially with their teams or boards. As a result, they often become emotionally guarded, which increases physiological stress and contributes to a nervous system stuck in high-alert mode.

Some of the most important breakthrough moments I've had with leaders, especially CEOs, come when they finally speak a quiet truth aloud: "I'm afraid." Afraid of failing. Afraid of letting people down. Afraid of damaging their reputation or not living up to expectations. This fear, when buried and unspoken, doesn't go away. It goes underground. And like most suppressed emotions, it finds a way out, often in unconscious, dysregulated behavior. Sometimes it leaks into the workplace through micromanagement, irritability, avoidance, or control. Other times, it shows up more acutely at home. That's why having a skilled coach, someone who's been in leadership and understands both the purpose and the pressure, is essential.

A *good* coach helps you slow down and pay attention to what's underneath the surface: your stress responses, your impact on others, and the fears that may quietly steer your behavior. More than that, a *great* coach helps you reconnect to your *why* and then align your intentions and actions from a centered, grounded place.

Intention followed by aligned action is everything. And that's good news. Because while you may not be able to control outcomes, market conditions, or other people's behavior, you can control your own actions, and you can practice showing up with awareness, with regulation, and with integrity. That is the power of leadership. We choose every day how we will interact with the world, and that choice, paired with the influence you hold, makes you a change agent. If you accept that role.

It's like I used to tell my children when they were young and heading out the door for school: "Don't forget to use your powers for good." And make no mistake: If you're a leader in a position of authority, you hold power, not just in your title but also in how much you influence others. Use it for good.

One of the most common blind spots I see in CEOs and leaders is a fundamental underestimation of their impact. You might think you're just offering a thought or checking in on a project, but your team is reading between every line. Your approval matters. Your reactions carry weight. People watch you closely, searching for cues about whether they're safe, trusted, or on the right path.

I once worked with the founder of a fast-growing startup who deeply valued staying close to his people and the work. He had a daily habit of walking around the office and stopping by employees' cubicles to ask about their projects, sometimes offering quick feedback or ideas. When he returned to his office, he felt great that he had made time to connect and show them that he cared, but his *impact* told a different story. What he thought was "helpful" feedback was often interpreted as a directive. Employees felt anxious and uncertain of whether or not they needed to change course or start something new.

As a result, managers found themselves having to react quickly to clarify what was actually expected and keep their reports on course. The CEO's simple check-in created unintentional chaos, frustration, and ultimately, dysregulation in others. This is the ripple effect. Even when your actions are well-intended, if you're not self-aware and attuned to your impact, you can unintentionally create confusion, fear, and disruption.

Now, don't get me wrong. I am in no way suggesting that trying to connect with others is a bad thing or discouraging leaders from getting close to the business, but being mindful of your positional power makes a huge difference. Let's imagine a more regulated version of that same interaction.

Before stepping into conversations with others, the CEO could pause and ask himself:

- *What is my intention in walking around today?*
- *What impact do I want to have?*
- *How do I want people to experience me in this moment?*

A quick reflection has the power to shift everything. In asking himself these questions, maybe he realizes his goal is simply to connect, to build morale, and to show appreciation, not to give feedback or problem-solve on the fly. From this place of clarity, he can move forward, fostering psychological safety rather than confusion. He might say to an employee, "I'm just here to check in. I'm not giving action items or changing direction. I'm just curious to hear what's on your mind." One sentence could disarm anxiety, clarify intent, and protect the trust between team members and their managers; if he had feedback, he could filter it through the appropriate channels, such as speaking with the individual's manager first.

This is what regulated leadership looks like in practice: self-awareness before interaction, clarity of intent, respect for structure, and a commitment to consistency. It's not about withholding input but stewarding your influence with care. When you take responsibility for how you're experienced, you stop unintentionally creating chaos and start cultivating trust. After all, your presence sets the emotional climate, and that climate shapes everything that grows underneath it.

I mentioned earlier that your energy is contagious. You may not realize it, but your presence speaks long before you say a word. The tension in your shoulders, the clipped tone in your voice, the urgency in your pacing, all of it sends signals to the people around you. Our brains are wired with what scientists call "mirror neurons," or cells that fire not only when we act, but when we observe *someone else* acting or emoting. These neurons are the foundation of empathy and social learning. When someone in a room is anxious or angry, our mirror neurons pick up on that and begin to mimic it, shifting our own emotional state in the process. This phenomenon is known as "emotional contagion," and leaders, whether they intend to or not, are among the most contagious people in any organization. That's why a dysregulated leader is dangerous.

When you lead from fear, aggression, or withdrawal, you unconsciously set that tone for everyone else. You don't have to tell your team how you're feeling; the way you show up does it for you. When your nervous system is in a state of protection, your leadership starts to operate from that same place: protective, reactive, defensive. You might micromanage. You might lash out. You might check out. You might stay busy but disengage. And the impact? Mistrust. Disconnection. Culture atrophy.

In a study done on emotional contagion, researchers found that "people automatically mimic the facial expressions, vocal tones, postures, and emotions of those around them, often within milliseconds," which leads to emotional convergence. This is why your inner state isn't just personal, it's organizational. Your nervous system leads your leadership, whether you're aware of it or not.

I'm sure by now you have thought of a few cringe-worthy moments where you, in a moment of dysregulation, have missed the mark. And while awareness is key, shaming yourself about these instances is wasted energy. A few moments of dysregulation don't define you or your leadership. What *does* is how you course-correct.

One of the most powerful and underestimated skills is knowing how to give an authentic apology. In my years of experience, I'm not sure I have ever seen a more powerful shift than the one that happens when a leader takes authentic accountability for their impact on others. It can be hard to do as it takes a great deal of self-awareness, humility, and vulnerability, which is why most leaders struggle with it. If you do decide to be one of the greats and courageously apologize when you miss the mark, make sure it is authentic, not performative or defensive. Name your impact, apologize, and then earn trust back by demonstrating values-aligned behavior moving forward.

As we've discussed, consistent, values-aligned behavior is what builds trust, which is the foundation of every successful relationship in business and in life. When people see that you're willing to pause, take ownership, and course-correct, it sends a powerful message: *I'm human and I'm committed to doing better.* That's regulation in action. And the more often you lead from that place, the more you build what I call "trust currency."

Think of trust currency like a bank account. Every time you show up with integrity (when your actions align with your words and your values), you make a deposit that teaches people what to expect from you. Over time, those small moments accumulate into something powerful: credibility, safety, and emotional margin. Why does this matter? Because even the most regulated leaders have moments when they miss the mark. You lose your cool in a meeting. You react too quickly to an email. You come across as more intense than you intended. But if you've built up enough trust currency, those moments are viewed in context. People think, *That's not like Sam. Something must be going on.* They give you grace. They assume positive intent. They see the misstep as an exception, not the rule. Of course, that doesn't mean you skip accountability. A true leader still owns the impact. But the apology lands differently because the trust is already there.

If you haven't built trust currency, if your behavior is inconsistent or misaligned with your stated values, the same missteps aren't dismissed. People don't assume you're having an off day; they assume that is who you are, and gossip, cynicism, and quiet disengagement grow. Eventually, the cost isn't just relational; it's cultural and organizational.

Trust currency is the product of regulated, intentional leadership. It's earned in moments of alignment and protected by authenticity and consistency.

Being a leader is a profound privilege, but it is not for the faint of heart. You're expected to absorb pressure, make tough calls, stay steady, and keep moving forward even when you're unsure or afraid. The higher you rise, the more your behavior is watched and mirrored, and the fewer people you can confide in. And yet, you are still a human being with a nervous system. Your heart still feels. Your body still responds to stress. And that stress, those feelings of fear, anxiety, and safety, don't just live in your mind. They are stored in your nervous system. That's why regulation isn't a luxury, but a lifeline.

You can't afford not to tend to your own internal state because how you show up has a profound impact on your business, culture, relationships, and life. You ripple out into every room, every meeting, and every decision.

This chapter is an invitation to check in with the ripple you're creating. Is it rooted in fear, reactivity, and pressure? Or is it shaped by presence, regulation, and intention? You don't have to do it perfectly, but you do have to do it consciously. The power of a regulated leader lies not in control but in congruence and in choosing, over and over again, to be the kind of leader who doesn't just perform well, but leads in a way that leaves others more whole, not more wounded. The people you are leading don't need you to be perfect. They need you to be present, honest, and regulated.

It truly does start at the top.

Reader Action:

1. When you are under pressure, which dysregulated leadership pattern do you default to: aggression, avoidance, control, withdrawal, or disengagement? Think of a specific situation where that pattern showed up. How did it impact others around you? What did it cost in terms of trust, clarity, or connection?

2. Identify one core value that feels most out of alignment when you are dysregulated. Get specific. What leadership behaviors in your life demonstrate this core value, and which behaviors contradict it?

CHAPTER 4

What Triggers Us Into Dysregulation

WE'VE TALKED ABOUT STRESS, pressure, and the impact of a dysregulated leader, but what throws us into dysregulation in the first place? Why is it that we can feel calm and clear one moment, and then in an instant, we feel our temperature rise, our heart beat faster, or our stomach turn, before we react? It happens to all of us. Leadership pressure is real and can be intense. Carrying the weight of an organization, a team, or a community and making decisions for its members leads to very real pressures, and while that pressure may be part of the job, few leaders are taught how to *carry* that pressure without leaking it onto others. The truth is that dysregulation doesn't start at work; it's a bit deeper than that.

We all have different triggers that push us into a reactive state and pull us out of balance. The root of an individual's dysregulation is personal and unique. Often, it's the result of lifelong emotional patterns formed in childhood that play out in both personal and professional contexts. We experience formative events, tell ourselves stories to make sense of them, and build beliefs that shape how we interpret stress and threat. These beliefs become patterns. Over time, the brain creates well-worn pathways that define how we react to discomfort, pressure, or conflict in our personal and professional lives. I've referenced the concept of being a whole leader. When it comes to this work, we have to remember that we are whole people, and our nervous systems don't clock out when we walk into the office.

The last few years have brought an intense convergence of pressure, both personal and professional, for all of us, creating massive ripple effects in many areas of our lives and society. At the time the COVID-19 pandemic hit, I was leading HR for another fast-growing biotech. We were scaling quickly, advancing our drug, and intentionally shaping a culture we believed was just as critical to our success as the science itself.

On the HR side of things, we had to quickly figure out remote work, navigate the complexity of hiring and onboarding in a virtual world, sustain high performance, and somehow continue building culture through a screen. Then came the policies, COVID protocols, vaccine mandates, mental health crises, and serious anxiety over inflation. Employees were asking, "What are you doing to support us?" Boards were asking, "How are you keeping top talent engaged and accountable?" On top of the pandemic, we were being called to address the social and political crises that emerged with full force: racial injustice, gender rights, women's reproductive rights, the war in Ukraine. Anxiety was everywhere. Employees were anxious. Leaders were anxious. And HR was expected to hold it all. But very few people stopped to ask how *we* were doing.

Many HR professionals burned out or left the function entirely. For me, it was also deeply personal, as my mom was just diagnosed with terminal breast cancer, and I was sending my last child off to college. I had to hold space for a stressed and grieving organization while managing my own. Yet, I am just one story in a sea of stories. Every person was experiencing not only the pressure inside work, but also all of the external pressure points they were bringing *into work*. It was, in every sense, a perfect storm. And in those conditions, dysregulation was inevitable. It showed up in meetings, in communication breakdowns, in team dynamics, and in how decisions were made. Looking back, I see so clearly how much our nervous systems matter, especially when we're leading through a crisis.

There are several common triggers that move us into a state of dysregulation; the first one, and the most common, is conflict. I always say culture is built on meaningful conversations: the ones we have and the ones we avoid. Conflict is something many of us want to avoid, and if it is unavoidable, we either approach it with aggressiveness and force or passiveness.

Years ago, I learned one of the most impactful leadership tools I had ever experienced, and to this day, it is the number one tool I coach on. Enter the "Drama Triangle." Originally created in the 1960s by Dr. Stephen Karpman, a psychiatrist and student of transactional analysis, the Drama Triangle is used to describe the roles people often unconsciously take on during conflict, and it has since been widely used in psychology, coaching, and organizational development to help individuals and teams recognize and shift out of dysfunctional relational patterns.

When I learned about the Drama Triangle, it was through an incredible mentor, Charlie Sheppard, Professor of Leadership, author of *Save the Drama for Your Mama*, and creator of the program *Leadership is a Choice*. Charlie adapted the Drama Triangle with a leadership focus, developing the Leadership Triangle as its counterpart, and integrating the concept of "locus of control" into both models. His work with the triangles had a profound impact on me, providing not only a practical tool to use in my work but also a framework to navigate conflict more effectively in every area of life. These models helped me reach a deeper level of self-awareness about my own tendencies in drama and offered clarity on how to overcome them.

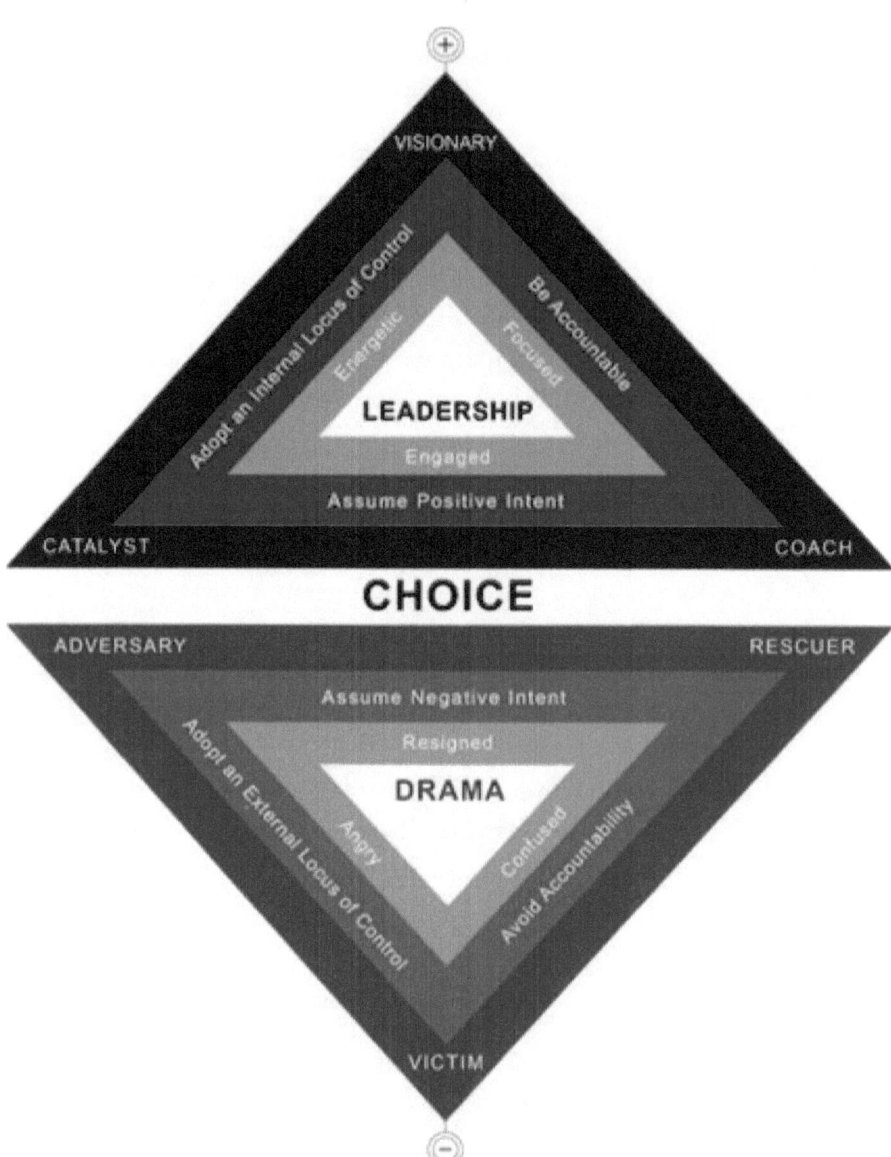

Let's start with understanding the Drama Triangle. There are three roles within the Drama Triangle: Victim, Rescuer, and Adversary, each representing a dysfunctional response to conflict. We all step into the drama triangle at times, and when we do, we automatically slip into one of these roles.

Below, I have included a short breakdown.

1. **Victim:**

   - Characteristics: Feels oppressed, helpless, powerless, and ashamed. Often seeks a rescuer to solve their problems and may not take responsibility for their situation.

   - Typical Statements: "Poor me!" "There's nothing I can do!" "Why does this always happen to me?"

2. **Rescuer:**

   - Characteristics: Feels a strong need to help others and often does so at their own expense. It can enable the victim's behavior by taking over their responsibilities.

   - Typical Statements: "Let me help you!" "I can fix this for you!" "You need me!"

3. **Adversary:**

   - Characteristics: Blames others, criticizes, and oppresses. They often exert control through anger, threats, and criticism.

   - Typical Statements: "It's all your fault!" "You're wrong!" "You need to do it my way!"

One of the biggest challenges of the Drama Triangle is how easily it can catch you off guard. Even after my years of teaching and coaching, I can still get caught in it. Sometimes, I find myself in all three roles, depending on the situation and my stress level, but most often, I tend to take on the Rescuer role. However, while the desire to show compassionate action and alleviate others' suffering is admirable and can be a strength when regulated, when dysregulated, it can create unintentional issues.

Consider the following scenario.

You are a manager and have assigned a task to one of your reports, Alex. Alex, unbeknownst to you, is feeling overwhelmed by his workload, as he's been given multiple projects with tight deadlines. He doesn't say anything to you when you give him the additional project, and instead, nods his head to confirm he's got it handled. Yet, little do you know, he's just placed you in the Adversary role.

Meanwhile, Alex goes to his colleague, Jamie, who often steps in to help Alex when he's overwhelmed. Alex assumes the Victim role and proceeds to tell her how overwhelmed he is and how unfair it is that you, his manager, assigned him new work. He says things like, "She doesn't even care about my stress level," and "I always get the toughest assignments."

Jamie, being the good and helpful colleague that she is, assumes the Rescuer role and tells Alex not to worry, that she will stay late and help him finish his tasks, stating, "You're right, it is unfair. You shouldn't have to deal with this alone."

The following day, Jamie comes to you directly and tells you that Alex is upset and thinks you don't care about his well-being. You, the manager, are offended and put off by how he can think such a thing. You've been trying so hard, and you can't understand why he chose to talk to others instead of coming to you directly. In that moment, from your perspective, you become the *Victim*, Alex becomes the *Adversary*, and Jamie is still trying to *Rescue* the situation.

Do you see how easy it is to step into? Without recognition, you will continue to circle the Triangle and move from one role to another.

To transition from the Drama Triangle, you must first understand the roles in the Leadership Triangle. Once you understand the roles and become aware of your own tendencies, you will be able to do so effectively. The three roles within the Leadership Triangle (Catalyst, Coach, and Visionary) are healthier, more regulated counterparts to the original roles. During the switch, typically:

- **Victim moves to Visionary:** Takes initiative to speak up, advocates for a compelling future, seeks solutions, and moves from helplessness to ownership.

- **Rescuer moves to Coach:** Empowers others to solve their own problems and offers support and inquiry instead of rescuing or over-functioning.

- **Adversary moves to Catalyst:** Frames the issues, allows others to see how they can contribute, and communicates expectations without blame or reactivity.

Let's examine the example above through the lens of the Leadership Triangle. What would a healthier, more regulated conversation between parties look like?

You, still the manager, have assigned a task to one of your reports, Alex, who is juggling multiple projects with tight deadlines and feels overwhelmed.

Jamie, the colleague who often jumps in to help, is aware of Alex's workload. But instead of stepping in to fix it all, she shifts from Rescuer to Coach, someone who supports others in finding their own solutions. She says:

> "That sounds like a lot, but I know you're capable. Have you had a chance to talk to our manager about what's on your plate? It might help to walk through what you need and what's realistic."

Instead of absorbing the emotional burden or doing the work herself, Jamie empowers Alex to advocate for himself. She trusts both him and the system to handle it maturely.

Because of this, Alex is able to move out of the Victim role and into the role of Visionary, someone who takes ownership of their experience and initiates honest dialogue. He schedules a quick meeting with you and says:

> "I want to make sure I can deliver high-quality work. With the current deadlines I'm managing, I'm feeling a bit stretched. Can we talk through priorities so I can execute well on this new project?"

You, instead of unknowingly stepping into the Adversary role, step into the role of Catalyst, someone who provides clarity and direction without defensiveness. You respond with:

> "Thank you for telling me. I didn't realize how much you had on your plate. Let's look at what's urgent and what can shift. I want you to feel supported and set up for success."

Alex feels seen and heard. There's no need for back-channel venting, no assumptions, and no blame.

The next day, there's no awkward confrontation or silent resentment. The team has modeled transparency, personal responsibility, and mutual respect: hallmarks of a regulated, values-based culture.

With intention and awareness, each person in this scenario stayed or shifted into a constructive leadership role. No one needed to be blamed or saved; instead, everyone took responsibility for their experience, leaned into clarity, and prioritized connection. This is the power of moving from Drama to Leadership.

Another important aspect of staying out of the Drama Triangle is understanding your "Locus of Control," or how you interpret the events around you and where you place responsibility. At its core, Locus of Control is about power, specifically, whether you believe that power lies within you or outside of you.

When you lead from an "External Locus of Control," you are in the Drama Triangle, and it often sounds like:

"There's nothing I can do."
"This always happens to me."
"They made me feel this way."

This mindset gives away your power. It keeps you in reactive mode, believing life happens *to* you and that you're just getting tossed around by circumstances, personalities, and politics. I've seen many dysregulated leaders get stuck here, especially when fear is in the driver's seat: fear of failure, fear of conflict, fear of being found out, or fear of disappointing others. They often end up blaming people, systems, or timing, and rarely pause to ask what is truly theirs to own.

On the other hand, leading from an "Internal Locus of Control" falls within the Leadership Triangle and is centered on agency. It doesn't mean pretending everything is in your control, but it does mean recognizing what is.

It sounds like:

> "I can't change the whole system, but I can choose how I respond."
> "I'm responsible for how I show up, even when things feel unfair."
> "I have choices, and I can take action aligned with my values."

Let's look at examples of each.

- External Locus of Control (Disempowered Leader/Drama Triangle):
  A department head is told by a peer that they're not perceived as collaborative. Instead of reflecting inward, they react defensively and blame the environment:

  "This company doesn't value strong voices. If you're direct, you get labeled as difficult."
  "They just don't get how much pressure I'm under. I don't have time to coddle everyone."

"That team never communicates clearly anyway, so of course it looks like I'm not collaborating."

In this example, the leader places responsibility for the situation entirely on others: the culture, the peer, the workload, or the other team's communication style. They perceive themselves as misunderstood and unfairly judged, and they fail to consider their role in the dynamic. There's no curiosity, no ownership, and no forward motion. As a result, the feedback becomes something to resent, not something to grow from.

- Internal Locus of Control (Empowered Leader/Leadership Triangle):
The department head receives the same challenging feedback, but the leader remains calm and regulated, leaning in with curiosity. When the feedback is delivered, instead of getting defensive or blaming the culture, they pause and reflect:

"I can't control how others perceive me, but I can control how I show up in meetings, how I listen, and how I follow through."

They take that feedback as an opportunity to lead more intentionally, reaching out to colleagues, clarifying shared goals, and inviting more feedback.

The externalized mindset keeps the leader stuck in the Drama Triangle, often toggling between Victim ("They're out to get me") and Adversary ("They're the problem, not me"). In contrast, an internal shift moves them into the Leadership Triangle as a Catalyst who owns their experience and actively creates change.

Understanding the difference between the Drama Triangle and the Leadership Triangle can change the way you view conflict. You will see it show up in your work relationships, personal relationships, politics, and any other dynamic involving human beings and dysregulation.

Other common triggers resulting in dysregulation or time in the Drama Triangle include:

- Communication Breakdowns
    - Misunderstandings or lack of clarity can quickly trigger fear, shame, or frustration. One of the largest contributors to misunderstandings is the use of technology. It is amazing what one short email, text, or instant message can do at the speed of light. One of my favorite examples of this is a story about the time I was coaching a COO who had a substantial workload, an intense communication style, and a high level of tenacity in getting things done. His positional power, combined with his natural style, gave him the reputation of being someone to be feared on his worst days and someone to avoid on his best.

        One day, he sent what he thought was a simple email to his project management team, asking for an update on a project timeline. The request was fair and logical, but with no context, a few rushed replies, and no tone to soften the urgency, it escalated fast. One team member felt blamed, another went silent, and a third forwarded the thread to their manager with a "Can you believe this?" pushing all three members of the team into the Drama Triangle.

        What could've been a ten-minute clarifying conversation fractured collaboration for weeks. No one was trying to create conflict, but the absence of clarity and connection opened the door. I always encourage leaders to pause before sending messages and reflect on their intent, desired outcome, and the level of relational focus required. Then they can decide whether or not the message would be better received as a phone call, Zoom, or face-to-face touch-base versus an email, text, or instant message.

- Fear of Failure or Loss of Control

    o Most of the individuals I work with in my coaching business are high achievers who exhibit some degree of perfectionism. These characteristics often lead people to internalize success or failure as personal identity, causing even small setbacks to feel threatening. They tend to be overly hard on themselves, which in turn leads them to be overly burdensome on others, either aggressively or passively. I was once tasked with delivering a high-stakes strategy off-site for a team struggling with trust and effectiveness. Pressure was high as the team was working on the company's most important deliverables. It was critical that they be able to work together and meet the aggressive milestones ahead, and if they continued functioning as they were, which was spending most of their time in the drama triangle, they would fail.

    The C-suite leader managing the team and requesting the offsite was an accomplished leader with the right intent. She had a clear vision for the outcome she wanted post-offsite, and we were aligned on the direction. The evening before the offsite, we had a final meeting that included the leader, the HR team, and a couple of other key members of her team who had contributed to planning the offsite. As we walked through the content of the meeting, I could sense the leader's anxiety; this offsite was critical for the company but also for her as a leader. As I discussed my approach, she launched at me, stating that team members had already been making comments that they didn't need to sit through an HR training and that they didn't believe it would be a valuable use of time. She criticized my content and openly expressed frustration about my approach. I knew that underneath that attack was fear: fear of losing control and credibility.

Her dysregulated energy shifted the energy in the entire meeting. At one point, I stopped her and assured her that I also wanted the offsite to be successful, that I had over twenty years of experience in leadership work, and believed it was going to be a productive meeting. Reminding her that I was not there to deliver an "HR training" but a strategic workshop tailored to address the team's specific needs. After the meeting ended, I was furious on the inside. Others in attendance came to ask if I was okay. I was, but they were not. They were rattled seeing two leaders, two colleagues, interacting that way. Shortly after the meeting, the leader called me to apologize. I accepted her apology and reassured her that the offsite would be great, and I'm happy to report that everyone remarked that it was one of the best workshops they had ever attended. To this day, they credit the workshop for moving them forward at a critical time. When fear takes over, it creates a ripple effect of dysregulation in you and those around you as you react. If the leader had remained regulated, it would have saved a great deal of stress, anxiety, and wasted time all around.

- External Pressures and Perceived Threats

    o In any leadership role, particularly at the CEO level, pressure is part of the deal. But it isn't just the internal pressures of building culture, managing employee expectations, making critical decisions, people management, etc., it's also the external pressures like investor expectations, board meetings, market shifts, talent shortages, and budget cuts that get the best of you. Pressure is often the invisible current running beneath your day, and unless you know how to release it, it starts to show up in subtle but costly ways. When external stress goes unprocessed, it doesn't just disappear; it leaks into your tone, your urgency, and your posture in meetings. It shows up as rushed decisions, clipped responses, or vague strategic shifts that leave your team wondering what just happened.

I was coaching a CEO of a fast-growing, high-tech startup who found himself in exactly this place. He was under an immense amount of pressure from his board, which was pushing him to cut costs and extend the company's cash runway, even if it meant laying people off. During our sessions, I watched the pressure he was under grow more intense and his anxiety around it increase.

On one particularly stressful day, he received scathing feedback from his board about missed revenue projections. The criticism cut deep, as he took it as a personal failure, and he was highly triggered, feeling a range of emotions like anger, frustration, and shame. He was dysregulated and, as a result, he shut down, deciding not to share the pressure he was experiencing with his leadership team and shoulder it on his own. In the weeks that followed, his internal meetings became more transactional. His presence grew quieter, but his urgency grew louder. He started making unilateral decisions, changing directions without explanation. His team didn't know what was going on, but they felt it. They felt the disconnection. The anxiety. The pressure to get it right without fully understanding what "right" even meant. Without meaning to, he created the very dynamic he was trying to avoid. Instead of rallying his team around a shared challenge, he made them feel uncertain, cautious, and sidelined.

This is a classic leadership paradox: In our effort to prevent conflict or failure, we often create the very conditions that lead to it. We avoid hard conversations, we micromanage, and we withdraw, and as a result, we create unstable environments. Pressure is real, but so is your choice in how you carry it. Regulated leaders don't ignore pressure; they transform it, name it, process it, and use it to bring people closer, not push them away.

So how do you know if you're leading from a dysregulated place? Sometimes, it's obvious. You snap at someone in a meeting. You can't sleep.

You obsess over a single email or rehearse a conversation in your head a dozen times. You ruminate over past mistakes and missteps. But more often, dysregulation is subtle. It hides under the surface of busyness and ambition. It wears the mask of urgency, accountability, and productivity. It feels like pressure, but it sounds like drive.

Here are some common signs that your nervous system, and therefore your leadership, might be dysregulated:

- You micromanage because you fear things slipping through the cracks.

- You avoid tough conversations, hoping the issue will resolve itself.

- You withdraw emotionally, becoming harder to read or connect with.

- You override your team's decisions instead of collaborating.

- You stay so busy putting out fires that you avoid your real priorities, especially your people.

- You feel like no one understands the pressure you're under, and you're carrying it alone.

- You hear yourself say, "I'll relax when this thing is over," but there's always another thing.

Let me be clear: These aren't character flaws. They're signs of a nervous system under stress. And the longer you stay in this mode, the more normalized it becomes, not just for you, but for those around you. It's impossible to eliminate pressure or emotion, but it is possible to build the awareness to recognize when you're leading from reaction instead of response, and to course-correct with intention instead of shame. What defines a regulated leader isn't whether they get triggered; it's how they respond when they do.

Below are a few core leadership behaviors that disrupt the cycle of dysregulation and reset the emotional tone with those around you.

- **Apology As Repair and Self-Awareness**
  A real apology is more than saying "I'm sorry." It's acknowledging impact and signaling accountability. It tells the people you impacted, "I see it, I own it, and I care enough to make it right."

- **Vision To Reorient**
  When chaos or fear creeps in, vision provides an anchor. Leaders who return to purpose, not just performance and productivity, help themselves and those around them move from reactivity back to alignment.

- **Clarity In Communication**
  Ambiguity breeds anxiety. Clear, honest, transparent communication, even when the news is hard, creates a sense of safety. Stay out of avoidance.

- **Forgiveness (of Self and Others)**
  Without forgiveness, shame lingers and resentment festers. Regulated leaders practice release, not just to move on, but to free up the energy needed to lead well.

- **Connection**
  Dysregulation thrives in isolation. But connection, checking in, and staying curious ground both the leader and the team in shared experience and trust.

When we are triggered, it's rarely just about the situation in front of us; often, it's about something older, like an unmet need or a pressure that hasn't been processed. Once we become aware of our triggers and patterns, the situations that pull us into dysregulation, we have a choice to make. Will we continue to repeat the pattern or disrupt it and choose a new way? Remember that you are responsible for your own choices, your own growth. Regulated leadership doesn't mean perfection; it means presence.

REGULATED LEADERSHIP DOESN'T MEAN PERFECTION, IT MEANS PRESENCE.

— *SAM WILLING*

Reader Action:

1. What situations or people tend to trigger you into dysregulation? Think back to a recent moment when you felt off and reactive. What fear or unmet need may have led to that response? How old is that strategy, and is it still serving you?

2. Make note of when you feel triggered for thirty days. For each moment of dysregulation, ask yourself:

    - *What was the trigger?*
    - *What was the story I was telling myself at that moment?*
    - *What was my reaction?*

Look for patterns, remember awareness is the first step in being able to create new patterns.

CHAPTER 5

How Regulation Forms Company Culture

"COMPANY CULTURE" HAS been a buzzword for several years, used by companies as a selling point for bringing in hot talent, differentiating themselves, and winning business. Yet, despite how often culture is discussed, many still misunderstand what culture is and how it's formed.

At its core, culture is the way people show up and behave consistently within a certain structure. Culture is found in families, churches, businesses, friend groups, and community groups, anywhere a group of people forms and establishes norms around interaction. It is built over time through consistent actions and behaviors. It is built in moments. Culture *always* forms. The question is whether it is happening by design or by default. When done well, culture becomes a company's competitive edge. When neglected or misaligned, it becomes a quiet but powerful force that can fracture trust, performance, and morale. A strong culture is built with great intention and care.

I have been brought into organizations in deep need of repair: cultures marked by anxiety, avoidance, and dysfunction. And while there is often enthusiasm around values and culture, most companies fall short in the follow-through. Leaders often get excited and define inspiring values, put them up on walls larger than life, and promote them on the website and recruiting videos, but rarely do they define how those values show up in day-to-day behaviors. Without clear alignment between values and actions, culture becomes ambiguous and accountability fades. When values are vague or ill-defined, pressure exposes the truth. Under stress, leaders often revert to dysregulated responses like micromanagement, avoidance, blame, or withdrawal that directly contradict the values they claim to uphold. The ripple effect is immediate: trust erodes, confusion spreads, and culture deteriorates.

It is important to note that culture changes over time as a company evolves. But as structures shift, systems change, and people come and go, values remain the anchor, and it is up to the leaders to embody those values consistently, especially under pressure.

Culture isn't owned by HR, nor is it maintained through perks or slogans. There's a collective responsibility to hold ourselves and others accountable for showing up in ways that are consistent with the culture we aspire to in every meeting, in every message, and in every moment of choice.

As we explored in the previous chapter, leaders set the tone, particularly in how they respond to pressure, feedback, and failure. When a leader's nervous system is dysregulated, the impact doesn't stop at their own decision-making. It permeates culture. It teaches people to be cautious, to avoid risk, and to retreat in self-protection. It creates a fight-or-flight response that hampers innovation, psychological safety, and trust.

One of the most extreme examples I've seen of dysregulation shaping culture was at a startup led by a CEO who, on the surface, said all the right things. He was an eternal optimist, charismatic, and clear about his commitment to the company's values of transparency and innovation. The company was moving fast, spending aggressively, and operating with ambitious timelines.

As is often the case in high-growth environments, the path to innovation naturally included risk, missteps, and failure. And to his credit, the CEO repeatedly told his people he welcomed bad news, dissenting opinions, and pushback, but his nervous system told a different story. When leaders brought concerns forward, especially about programs not performing well or key targets being missed, he often responded with denial, defensiveness, and visible frustration. Sometimes it showed up subtly in a dismissive tone or body language that signaled his disinterest and disengagement. Other times, it was overt: blaming, finger-pointing, or shutting down the conversation entirely.

Over time, despite his well-crafted messaging, his emotional responses trained the organization to protect him from the truth, resulting in silence. Teams stopped surfacing critical risks. Conversations moved to the "watercooler," where people vented in hushed tones about the growing disconnect between what the CEO said and how he acted. They spoke of his "toxic optimism," a phrase that surfaced again and again. And they learned, without anyone formally saying it, that dissent was dangerous and that full honesty came with consequences.

The culture shifted in subtle, then seismic ways. People stopped challenging ideas. They filtered their updates. Some avoided meetings altogether, preferring to work around the problem rather than through it. Innovation slowed. Accountability dropped. Productivity suffered. But the more devastating impact was financial. Because critical information wasn't shared candidly with the CEO, costly mistakes weren't caught early. Money was wasted at a time when the company desperately needed to conserve cash. Ultimately, the company failed, running out of time and money. Was the dysfunction in the culture solely responsible? It would be hard to say, given the many uncontrollable factors involved, but it certainly didn't help.

This is the quiet danger of how dysregulation can impact culture. While the CEO projected confidence and positivity, what he modeled, especially under pressure, was something else entirely. The culture that formed wasn't based on values. It was based on emotional avoidance. It was a culture where people avoided conflict and withheld information unless it was packaged perfectly.

This is how culture forms, not from what we say when things are going well, but from how we show up in high-pressure moments. Without regulation, fear takes the wheel. And when fear takes over, trust begins to erode.

> TRUST IS YOUR **BELIEF** IN MY **INTEGRITY**, MY **ABILITY**, MY **RELIABILITY**, MY **STRENGTH**, AND THAT I AM TELLING YOU THE **TRUTH** - AND MY BELIEF IN THE SAME IN YOU.
>
> — DR. ROB MCKENNA

Trust isn't just a "nice-to-have," it's the foundation everything else stands on. We are all people working in systems. Be it a family system, a work system, or a community system, organizational systems are a way of life, and how healthy and effective they are depends on the level of trust between the people within them. Within a company, it's about whether employees believe that their leaders will tell them the truth, keep their word, and make decisions that honor the whole, not just the few.

In 2025, WiLD Leaders, a research-based leadership firm focused on whole and intentional leadership development, released the WiLD Leaders State of Trust at Work Report, consisting of fifteen years of research and data regarding trust across many organizations. Using this research as a foundation, the WiLD team built the WiLD Trust Index, a groundbreaking tool enabling organizations to measure trust in three areas: personal, team, and organizational.

First, the study confirmed that trust is a leading indicator of performance and can not only be measured, but also be built intentionally. It is not an intangible idea or feeling but a measurable outcome based on consistent leadership and organizational behaviors that are directly linked to business success and personal wellness.

Second, one of the most intriguing findings had to do with personal trust. Dr. Rob McKenna, Founder of WiLD Leaders, has this to say about personal trust: "Personal trust is about growth, not perfection. It requires self-awareness to identify our strengths and weaknesses, a commitment to continuous improvement, and the ability to act authentically in alignment with our values. This foundation lays the groundwork for the confidence, vulnerability, and consistency needed to foster trust at the team and organizational levels. When we prioritize building trust in ourselves and being trustworthy people, we create a ripple effect that positively influences our interactions with others. We show up with confidence and authenticity, ready to navigate the complexities of trust in teams and organizations."

Simply put, trust always starts with self-awareness, which is achieved, in part, by establishing personal trust. The study highlighted three key drivers to doing this:

1. **Self-differentiation**, or the ability to be both clear about one's identity and values while maintaining strong, caring connections with others.

2. **Meaning and productivity**, or the extent to which one feels their work is meaningful and productive.

3. **Awareness**, or the understanding of one's competence, motivations, and support needed for success, and how one reacts in high-pressure situations.

Finally, another key finding that excited me was that composure under pressure is also a key driver of trust. As mentioned previously, being able to stay steady and regulated during high-pressure situations has a direct impact on those around you and the culture you aspire to build. If you react instead of respond, if you allow fear and anxiety to drive the bus, trust can deteriorate quickly.

But while breakdowns in trust and culture can be destructive, they are not always permanent.

I've also had the privilege of working with a CEO who, during a time of high pressure both personally and professionally, chose to course-correct with vulnerability and authenticity, resulting in a profound impact on herself and her entire organization. I had worked with her for some time and considered her one of the strongest CEOs I'd ever coached. It was her first time in the top role, and she brought not only the competence and industry respect for the job but also a deep heart for leadership. A former competitive swimmer with a two-decade corporate career behind her, she had a remarkable capacity for pressure and performance.

During her second year leading the company, she was diagnosed with thyroid cancer. Fearing that her diagnosis would lead others to question her ability to lead, she did what many high-performing leaders do: she compartmentalized. She took calls from her doctor in the car, wiping away tears before re-entering the office. She scheduled her surgery for the minimum time away and wore a scarf to cover the scar. She soldiered on, believing she was protecting the company by shielding her struggle. When she came to me for coaching, she told me something that struck a deep chord.

Despite her commitment to being a servant leader, someone who leads with purpose and people at the center, she felt the culture wasn't evolving into what she'd envisioned. Something was off. She couldn't quite name it, but there was a disconnect between her values and the cultural tone of the company. We started by exploring her *why*, her identity, and the fears she hadn't spoken aloud. And then came the clarity.

She realized that the culture she wanted, one of high trust, authenticity, and transparency, had been unintentionally contradicted by her own behavior. By hiding her story, she had modeled silence over openness and protection over trust. So, I encouraged her to share her experience with her leadership team during a trust reset offsite we were planning together, and she did. With courage and composure, she told her story, acknowledging the fear that led her to keep it private, and apologized for not trusting the team to have her back. Then, she made a clear commitment: "That's changing today. I want to lead differently, and I want us to build something stronger together."

The response was extraordinary. Not only did she receive a wave of support, but she also broke the barrier around humility and vulnerability in a way that created new space for everyone else to show up more honestly. From that point on, her presence shifted, as did the culture. People began speaking more freely. Trust began to rebuild. And most importantly, the team felt seen, valued, and safe.

As you now know, culture is built on meaningful conversations, the ones we have *and* the ones we avoid, and avoidance is one of the largest contributors to the deterioration of trust in any relationship. When we avoid hard conversations, others fill in the gaps with assumptions that are rarely generous, incredibly distracting, and serve to undermine performance.

To help leaders foster a healthy culture and trust, I coach them to lead with the **4 C's of Culture:**

1. **Curiosity:** Seek to understand, not assume.

2. **Courage:** Be willing to have the conversation, even when it's hard.

3. **Connection:** Show up human, acting relationally before transactionally.

4. **Compassion:** Lead with care for yourself and others.

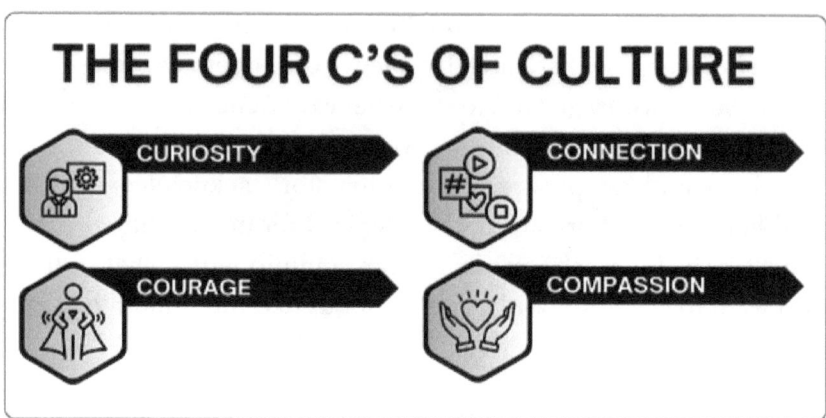

These aren't soft skills but strategic behaviors that build the foundation for innovation, clarity, and cohesion in your culture, and they require regulation. Without self-awareness and nervous system regulation, we default to fear, avoidance, or reactivity.

Culture isn't what you say it is. It's what people feel: in meetings, in moments of feedback, and in how leaders handle pressure and presence. It's an outcome of your collective behaviors, repeated over time, and the emotions those behaviors elicit in others. Regulated leadership isn't a "nice-to-have;" it's the stabilizing force that connects your values to your impact and your strategy to your culture.

Reader Action:

1. How are your behaviors influencing the culture forming at your organization? Think of a recent situation where your presence, regulated or dysregulated, had a ripple effect on your team. What energy did your actions send, and how aligned was it with the culture you want to create?

2. Choose one of the 4 C's of Culture and commit to embodying it more intentionally for one week. Before meetings or interactions with others, ask yourself:

   - *What does this value in action look like today?*
   - *How do I need to regulate myself to show up that way consistently?*

At the end of the week, reflect on how being more intentional shifted the dynamics and/or outcome of your interactions with others.

CHAPTER 6

The Role of Compassion and Self-Compassion

IT MIGHT NOT BE what you expect in a leadership book, but yes, compassion gets its own chapter. And if you know me, this isn't a surprise. Compassion is the thread that runs through almost everything I do, whether I'm coaching an executive, volunteering, navigating family life, or having honest conversations with friends. It's more than a value for me; it's a way of being.

I first discovered the power of compassion early in my career, during a season when I felt deeply out of place in a traditional corporate system. It wasn't just a word I stumbled upon but something I lived and felt, something that shifted how I showed up and how I wanted to lead.

I had just started a manager-level HR role at a fast-paced biotech company. During my first week, I was tasked with firing an employee who had not been performing well in her role for quite some time, and the organization had decided it was time for her to leave. I read through the documentation and met with her manager, as well as my own, a highly experienced older gentleman with traditional views of hierarchy. He explained exactly how the process would go. I was to meet with the employee and her manager to communicate her termination, walk her to her desk, stand over her as she cleared out her belongings, and then escort her out of the building.

As I entered the conference room and sat across from the employee, something didn't feel right. I knew letting her go was the right move, but as it came to my turn to talk, to guide her through what would happen next, my heart stepped in. I saw her eyes looking back at me, anxious and embarrassed. But instead of walking her to her desk as directed, I told her that she was free to leave and that I would be happy to make arrangements for her to come in after hours and get her things.

When I relayed this decision to my manager, he was visibly frustrated, letting me know that that wasn't how things were done and that no one was going to want to come in after hours and meet her. To this, I said I would, and that weekend, I left my family and drove the thirty minutes to the office to meet her and help her clear out her things. When we were finished, she looked at me with tears in her eyes and thanked me for not embarrassing her during work hours, and we said goodbye. Several months later, she reached out to let me know she had landed a new job that she loved.

That was a defining moment for me in my career and my life, as I realized how much compassion can shape someone's experience and how deeply it matters. From that day on, I committed to bringing compassion into my work as intentionally as I did in my personal life.

That was only the first of many terminations I would have to facilitate in my career. At one point, a CEO even told me that I was particularly "gifted" at it. That so-called compliment gave me pause, as I was fully aware of the disconnect between my compassionate heart and my desire to help others, and the act of firing. The irony was not lost on me. Still, I understood what he meant. I had found a way to hold space for someone's dignity, even while delivering difficult news. That did not mean people always received it with grace. Many did not. More often, they walked away with disdain for me, even though my role was that of a messenger and rarely the actual decision-maker. It could be rough on my empath's heart. I cried after most terminations, not because I believed the decision was wrong, but because of the impact I had on another human being's life.

Through reflection, I've come to understand that what made me good at it wasn't a lack of emotion or toughness, but the presence of compassion. Even when someone's behavior was challenging and the situation was messy, I chose to lead with humanity. These experiences, while difficult, shaped what I now consider to be my core beliefs about people, the lens through which I lead, coach, and live.

1. All human beings are imperfect and yet capable of greatness.
2. We all long to be valued.
3. Compassion is the key to meaningful change.

When I hold these at my center, I'm able to respond to others with grace and compassion, even when, especially when, it's hard.

The word "compassion" is often misunderstood, perceived as soft or weak in some way. However, compassion is quite the opposite. It is a word associated with incredible strength and action, and where we connect our head, heart, and hands. The definition of compassion is to experience another person's suffering and take action to ease their pain, and it is different from sympathy or empathy because it is action-oriented.

Let's break that down a bit further. "Sympathy" means feeling bad for someone, "empathy" means feeling bad *with* someone, and compassion is feeling bad *with* someone and then *taking action to ease their suffering*.

Imagine walking down the street and someone falls down to the ground in front of you. If you had sympathy, you might say, "That's awful. How embarrassing," and keep walking. If you had empathy, you might say, "That's awful. I can imagine how embarrassing that would be. I hope they aren't hurt," and keep walking. But if you had compassion, you would say, "That's awful. I can imagine how embarrassing that would be. I hope they aren't hurt," and then extend your hand to help them up. You see, the only thing that changes that person's situation is the extended hand, the lift up.

Several years ago, empathy got all the buzz. According to leadership experts and mental health advocates, we know that we should be empathetic, but empathy alone is not enough. If we stop at empathy, we stop just short of meaningful change. Compassion is the key to meaningful change. It's not enough to feel; we must do.

We're living in a time when we need "doing," when we need courageous people to stand up and take action to ease the suffering of others. The landscape of leadership and life has gotten more complex over the last few years, and the issues organizations and their employees face are vast and unsettling. The worlds of work and life are intertwined more than ever before. We are moving fast, rushed, distracted, dysregulated, often missing opportunities to show compassion to others, and we are short on time and energy. We've talked a lot about culture in this book, and the truth is that compassionate leadership is a necessity. Compassion shifts organizations; it creates psychological safety, fuels innovation, strengthens trust, and boosts retention and productivity.

According to a study (Hougaard, 2021), compassionate leaders are perceived as more competent, a powerful reminder that compassion and effectiveness are not opposites; they're partners. Compassionate leadership builds deep, meaningful relationships that drive loyalty and increase an organization's capacity to navigate change. It also creates a culture where trust isn't just a value but an experience, even in the hardest seasons.

One very important thing to note about authentic compassion is that, like many things, it must start with the self. Self-compassion is the key to being able to authentically extend compassion to others, as we cannot offer others something we don't already have.

This is a concept so many of my clients, and people in general, struggle with, including myself. The world is not a compassionate place. From a young age, we are inundated with messages about pushing ourselves and giving one hundred percent, and are trained to be hypercritical of ourselves and others, always comparing, striving, and swirling around in perfectionism.

High-achievers have a particularly challenging time with self-compassion. Most of them have spent their lifetime and career in performance mode, believing that a requirement of success is force and struggle, which results in feelings of inadequacy, even in the midst of worldly success. When clients get real about the ways they talk to themselves, the shame and guilt they wear, and the lack of rest and recovery in their lives, it breaks my heart. Often, all of these habits have led to an overly harsh existence in their own minds, harsh as it relates to themselves and others.

A level of bitterness and resentment has settled into their hearts, and without even realizing it, they find themselves easily frustrated by others' imperfections or need for rest. Once they begin to understand the role of compassion in their business and performance, and accept the theory that it must start with self, I see transformational changes take place as they make peace with the reality that they are high-achieving, performing, driven human beings and are still imperfect, as we all are.

I've had the privilege of walking side by side with them as they counter the lies and criticisms that have many times been in their minds for years, and they replace them with more loving truths. I see how it makes a difference in their own confidence levels and how it spills out into all of their relationships, business and personal.

When we criticize ourselves, we also tend to criticize others. Think about how you talk to yourself. Are you critical? Do you hold yourself to a level of perfectionism? Would you talk to a good friend like you talk to yourself? And if you did, would you have any friends left? Self-compassion is not a pity party. I am not saying you shouldn't hold yourself to high standards, but there is a profound difference between perfectionism, which impedes performance, and excellence, which drives it.

I will never forget an interaction I had with a colleague a few years ago. We were both executives, women, and mothers. We often talked about juggling it all and the craziness of the environment we were in, but we were very different in our approaches to life. She lived in a state of reactivity and was extremely hard on herself and others. She lacked self-compassion and, as a result, often criticized and grew frustrated with people, which led to consistent relationship flare-ups.

One morning, we had an executive meeting scheduled. When this colleague walked into my office to greet me, her face was completely swollen and bruised. She told me she had been on a bike ride earlier that morning and had crashed into a parked car. I felt a wave of empathy for her and asked why she came in. From my perspective, the logical and most compassionate thing to do would have been to stay home and rest after something so traumatic. She said she felt it was important to have face time with the CEO to show how engaged she was, since she was hoping for a promotion. As she turned and walked away from me, I saw it: a big black tire mark down the back of her calf.

I sat there thinking, *Why do we do this to ourselves?* Why do we have so little compassion for ourselves that we continue pushing forward, even when our bodies and minds are clearly signaling us to stop? Her decision wasn't just self-harming; it sent a powerful message to everyone watching. It modeled a version of leadership built on self-sacrifice, fear, and perfectionism, not one rooted in presence, humanity, and trust. When leaders can't extend compassion inward, it often leaks outward as criticism, control, or detachment. This erodes psychological safety and hurts performance across the board. High-achieving, self-critical leaders don't just burn themselves out; they create pressure-cooker cultures where others also struggle to thrive. Self-compassion, on the other hand, becomes a foundation for grounded leadership: one that creates clarity, fosters healthy ambition, and drives sustainable results.

That's why I've always been drawn to redemption stories, moments where compassion interrupts the cycle of pressure and perfection and creates space for a different kind of growth: one that is honest, human, and performance-enhancing at its core. I've witnessed these stories unfold in the most unexpected places. People on the brink of burnout who, when met with empathy instead of shame, rise stronger, clearer, and more effective. Compassion makes room for change, not just emotionally, but operationally; it opens up the possibility for repair, realignment, and renewed purpose.

As an HR leader, I've long believed that one of the most impactful things a leader can do is take the anxiety out of work for others. When people feel safe, they think more clearly, contribute more fully, and connect more deeply with the mission. What if you looked at your organization through that lens? What if performance wasn't only about pushing harder but also about reducing unnecessary friction? What if leadership meant not just driving results, but alleviating suffering? Compassion isn't soft; it's strategic. And when applied well, it becomes one of the most powerful drivers of trust, engagement, and sustainable success.

But how do you actually build a compassion practice, and what does it look like to live and lead with compassion at the center? The encouraging news is that, like gratitude, compassion is a muscle. And like any muscle, it gets stronger with consistent, intentional use.

Building compassion starts with self-awareness. It requires slowing down long enough to notice your own patterns, especially the ones that show up when you're tired, stressed, or afraid. As a leader, your ability to regulate yourself and extend compassion to *yourself* is the foundation for how authentically you can extend it to others. When you begin to recognize your own emotional cues and tend to them with care instead of criticism, you naturally become more grounded, more generous, and more effective in how you support those around you.

Here are a few simple but powerful ways to build a self-compassion practice:

1. **Speak kindly to yourself.** Replace your inner critic with the voice of a trusted friend, someone who sees your heart and your effort.
2. **Practice mindfulness.** Create space for quiet through prayer, meditation, or journaling. Focus on themes like gratitude, forgiveness, and compassion.

3. **Rest.** When you're depleted, honor your body, mind, and spirit with rest instead of pushing harder.

4. **Forgive yourself.** Release the weight of guilt or shame from past mistakes. Imperfection is part of being human.

5. **Engage in self-care.** Prioritize simple acts that help you feel grounded: a walk in nature, a good book, deep breaths.

6. **Reflect on your strengths.** Write down what you like about yourself, and revisit moments when others have affirmed your gifts.

7. **Ask for support.** Don't suffer in silence. It takes courage to say, "I need help."

8. **Celebrate the small wins.** Notice when you choose compassion, for yourself or others, and name it. Maybe it's a boundary you held, a thought you shifted, or simply the choice of rest over hustle.

Each of these practices is a step toward cultivating a more compassionate way of being, one that strengthens not just your leadership but your humanity.

One of the most powerful questions a coach ever asked me was this: "How are you participating in your own suffering?"

It stopped me in my tracks and forced me to pause and reflect on the ways I was limiting and hurting myself, most of which traced back to a lack of self-compassion and an unrelenting pursuit of perfection.

Remember the text story? The one where I accidentally sent a message meant for my husband to the CEO? In that moment, I had to dig deep. I was flushed, embarrassed, and swimming in self-judgment and anxiety. But I knew I couldn't stay there. I had to move through it with intention, accountability, and a whole lot of self-compassion, not just for my own sake, but for the sake of the organization and the relationships that mattered. Staying stuck in shame would've served no one. But moving forward from a grounded place of compassion? That's leadership. That's regulation. And that's the work. When we are intentional about compassion, we heal and help others heal, too.

Compassion is contagious. Research shows that witnessing an act of compassion or kindness increases the likelihood that the observer will act kindly themselves by up to eighty-seven percent. But here's the key: In order to make a change, we must slow down long enough to see people clearly. To witness the suffering and then be willing to take compassionate action to make a change.

Compassion becomes much simpler when we slow down and operate from a grounded, regulated space. It's what allows us to hold people accountable without breaking their spirit. It's what grounds us when pressure mounts, and what connects us when things fall apart. And it starts with you. When you treat yourself with compassion, you model a more human way to lead. You make it safe for others to be honest, to take risks, and to recover from failure. In a world that often values perfection over presence, compassion becomes your greatest advantage. I truly believe that if we can get to a point where compassion for self and others is consistent with how we show up in the world, we can change the world.

Reader Action:

1. When was the last time you offered yourself compassion in a moment of failure, disappointment, or embarrassment? What did you say to yourself, or what do you wish you had said? How would your leadership shift if you spoke to yourself with the same kindness and encouragement you use with others?

2. This week, practice replacing your self-critical thoughts with more self-compassionate truths. Write down each time you do this, and at the end of the week, reflect on how this practice influenced your interactions with others.

CHAPTER 7

How Regulation Builds Resilience

WE HAVE HEARD A LOT about the word "resilience" over the last several years, as it relates to life and leadership. Many leadership books, workshops, and coaching programs are built around being a resilient leader, as more CEOs and HR teams invest in strategies and employee benefits that claim to boost resiliency in individuals and cultures. Building resilient workplaces has become big business, but there are some missing links to what most of us have been taught that, if left unaddressed, will set us up for a never-ending pursuit of resilience without ever truly building it.

Resilience is often described as our ability to bounce back from hardship, to be able to adapt, to stay steady in storms, and to grow stronger through struggle, but resilience is also increasing our capacity for experiencing joy and is strongly linked to regulation. When you build resilience, you're actively strengthening your nervous system, your mental outlook, and your emotional well-being.

Research consistently shows that resilient individuals experience lower rates of anxiety and depression, improved cardiovascular health, stronger immune response, and greater life satisfaction. Resilient leaders recover faster, think more clearly under stress, and respond instead of reacting. When we practice and improve our ability to regulate our nervous systems, we have access to a wider range of emotional and physiological tools that help us stay grounded under pressure and re-center more quickly when knocked off course.

As we discussed earlier in the book, our nervous system plays a central role in how we experience and respond to stress. Resilience isn't about eliminating stress, but about how we relate to it. And the more regulated our nervous system, the more capacity we have to face adversity without shutting down, lashing out, or spiraling, and the more capacity we have for experiencing joy.

In Chapter 2, we discussed the autonomic nervous system and the two systems included within it: the sympathetic and the parasympathetic. When these branches are in balance, you toggle back and forth between both systems with flexibility and are able to exhibit emotional regulation, allowing you to feel emotions fully without being overtaken by them.

People with resilience don't avoid their emotions; they ride the wave of them with certainty that they will pass, maintaining confidence that they will be able to get back to functioning well quickly, despite whatever comes their way. It is not a belief that things will go perfectly or even smoothly all of the time; in fact, individuals with high levels of resilience have experienced and accepted that life involves some level of suffering and loss, but they have built enough trust in themselves to respond with courage, clarity, and care, no matter the outcome.

We have talked about the concept of self-trust throughout the book, which is an essential part of effectively regulating your nervous system. Without it, challenges can often feel like threats, and you will be challenged to stay steady, make decisions that align with your values, and recover when things don't go as planned. But with it, the same challenges present opportunities for learning, alignment, and growth.

This is where resilience and regulation meet. Regulated leaders can access their self-trust more easily because their nervous system isn't hijacked by fear or reactivity. When you are regulated, you can pause, reflect, and respond with intention. Each time you do this, your self-trust gets stronger. I see this all of the time in my work. When I am working with leaders with a tendency to avoid conflict, we work on equipping them with the tools needed to navigate challenging conversations. Once they start having them and realize they can come out on the other side lighter and more confident, they build self-trust in their ability to have them more often. It doesn't mean they will enjoy them, but that they recognize that the energy they carried around these conversations in the past was harmful and approach them from a regulated state.

In Chapter 3, we discussed the concept of Internal and External Locus of Control, which is another key layer to resilience. When we operate from an External Locus of Control, we believe we are at the mercy of circumstances and that things happen to us. When we shift to an Internal Locus of Control, where resilient leaders operate, we are able to find calm and respond instead of react.

Resilient leaders are not in denial about challenges, but they do not allow themselves to get stuck in blame, helplessness, or avoidance. They slow down and ask themselves key questions such as: *What is mine to own here?* and, *Where do I have influence and agency?* This allows them to be solution-oriented, empowered, and able to move forward with decisiveness and purpose rather than force. It is important to recognize when you are stepping into dysregulation, feeling overwhelmed, or becoming triggered, and then take a purposeful pause. We must stop outsourcing our emotional state to others and circumstances and instead focus on what we can choose, control, and shift.

One of the most powerful ways to build resilience is by intentionally doing hard or uncomfortable things. Resilience is like a muscle; it strengthens through use and develops over time. When we step into the uncomfortable, we stretch our physical, emotional, and psychological capacity.

A few months after I lost my mom, I heard about a program called Men and Women of Discomfort, a program centered around embracing discomfort and habit stacking in community. When you commit to the program, you agree to do several daily habits each day for ninety days, such as eating only whole foods, drinking ninety-six ounces of water per day, getting seven hours of sleep each night, working out daily, and checking in with the

MWOD community to take account of how you are progressing. In addition, new habits are added each week for the first several weeks.

Most join MWOD for the physical aspect, with the desire to get in the best shape of their life, but I joined to build self-trust and resilience. I wanted to overcome some of the old talk tracks in my head around perfectionism, discipline, follow-through, and discomfort. I had big goals for my coaching and leadership business, and I knew it would require a more confident, self-assured version of myself. I also knew I had some heavy grief to work through.

Many people in my life thought I was crazy for joining MWOD. After all, it is a very strict program, and I have always taken my health seriously, stayed in good shape. And I chose to begin it during the holidays of all times. I got a lot of flak for that, which became an exercise in discomfort, especially for me as a people pleaser who does not like to be criticized.

The program proved to be one of the most challenging things I have ever done. I was not perfect, which is part of the point, but I did it and finished strong, feeling more mentally, physically, and emotionally resilient than I ever had. The most difficult aspects of the program for me were the silent meditation, the cold showers, and sitting through social situations where I was eating different food and abstaining from alcohol.

On the last day of the program, there was a challenge that lasted for a few hours and included several activities that were not only physically demanding but also mentally difficult. These included running outside in the cold, long silent meditations, and an incredible number of lunges, push-ups, and squats. We happened to be in Sun Valley, Idaho, at the time, and it was freezing cold with snow on the ground. As I was running outside, I remember thinking, *I can't believe I'm doing this. A year ago, I never would have been doing this. I would have been inside drinking coffee in my pajamas.*

I felt so proud of myself with the realization that I had, in fact, become a woman who does hard things, who follows through on promises to herself, and who has agency in her life.

MWOD is not for everyone, but for me, it opened a door to healing. Embracing discomfort changed my mind, my body, and my nervous system. I learned how to trigger my fight-or-flight and bring myself back to a place of calm by activating my parasympathetic system through practices like breathwork, mindfulness, and gratitude. Every time I stepped into the freezing cold shower, I was triggered, telling myself I was doing it because I said I would, I would yelp and then breathe through the rest of the time, sometimes turning on a great song and dancing, other times just closing my eyes and breathing. Now I can get into a cold plunge; it isn't ever easy or something I want to do, but when I get in, I remind myself that I'm doing it because I said I would, and I am a woman who does hard things and follows through on promises to herself.

Each time we face difficulty and stay present instead of avoiding, numbing, or reacting, we teach our nervous system that we can be uncomfortable and still calm, still safe. Over time, this reduces our reactivity and increases our window of tolerance and adaptation, both hallmarks of a regulated and resilient leader.

Embracing discomfort, doing hard things is often a catalyst for massive growth and refinement. Many leaders have expressed that their most difficult seasons were also the most formative and full of growth. It is through these difficult seasons that their values are clarified, their character is strengthened, their strengths are revealed, and their connection to purpose is magnified and renewed. Of course, all of this formation and growth is dependent on how we approach challenging times. We have complete responsibility for how we show up and interact with the world. When we approach challenging times with an internal locus of control, vulnerability, and a commitment to growth and curiosity about what's possible, we build trust not only in ourselves but in others, and we realize we are not alone. And realizing you're not alone is often a deep unmet need for so many leaders.

Resilience is a significant leadership differentiator. In fact, McKinsey & Company (2022) reported that *"resilience is one of the most critical leadership capabilities in today's environment of rapid change and disruption."* Leaders with high resilience typically model emotional steadiness during change and uncertainty, inspire greater confidence, and foster cultures of authenticity, adaptability, and learning.

Many organizations I have worked with express a desire to increase psychological safety. "Psychological safety" is the belief that it is safe to speak up, make mistakes, and be yourself without fear. High-trust environments cultivate high psychological safety. Leaders who build their own skills around regulation and who intentionally respond to mistakes or feedback with curiosity instead of shame, and steadiness instead of reactivity, set a powerful tone.

Now, let's revisit joy and the importance of pursuing it, especially in hard times, to strengthen our nervous system and our resilience.

Many of the CEOs I work with will admit something they'll never say in the boardroom: They wish they experienced more joy in their day-to-day work. For these high-performing, highly competent leaders who have achieved what many only dream of, joy feels just out of reach. And it's not because they don't love what they do. It's because the weight of responsibility, the pace of decisions, and the unrelenting demands of leadership leave little space to savor the good. What I've learned, and what research from Brené Brown and others affirms, is that joy isn't a byproduct of success. It's an intentional practice.

Joy, like compassion, is one of those words we don't often use in business settings. It can feel too emotional, too soft, and too indulgent for a quarterly earnings call. Many leaders I coach avoid the word entirely, even though they long for the experience. Why? Because joy feels vulnerable. As Brené Brown says, "When we lose our tolerance for vulnerability, joy becomes foreboding." We start to believe it's safer to keep our expectations low and to brace for impact rather than savor the moment. But this guarded posture, this constant bracing, robs us of the very resilience we need to lead well.

In thinking about this, it's important to remember that joy is not the same as happiness. Happiness is often tied to outcomes: hitting a target, winning the deal, securing the funding. Joy, on the other hand, is deeper. It's a state of being grounded in meaning, presence, and connection. Typically, we experience joy when we're aligned with our values, when we slow down enough to notice the beauty of what we've built and the humanity of the people we lead, and reconnect with our purpose. Recently, I was on a coaching call with a leader who was feeling overwhelmed by so many things around him, namely the state of the world. He voiced that he was having a difficult time coming out of his funk, even after trying many of the regulation techniques we had previously focused on, so I encouraged him to seek joy in small things. Taking my suggestion, he made the choice to buy a last-minute ticket to a concert that night. I was so happy to hear this choice that he made and encouraged him to be aware of the suffering in the world and keep an eye out for ways to help, but also to lean into joy, to reconnect, and find a space of gratitude.

Oftentimes, a simple act like this can break the cycle of overwhelm and get us moving in the right direction. It doesn't alleviate suffering, but it does remind our nervous system that joy is possible even in the midst of it. We don't need to keep ourselves buried in the suffering and the hard; we can hold both the suffering and pursue joy at the same time, and without guilt.

So how do we lean into joy in the midst of suffering? Just like empathy is the gateway to compassion, gratitude is the gateway to joy and the practice that makes it possible. In Brené Brown's twelve-year research project with eleven thousand data points, she found something counterintuitive: "It's not joy that makes us grateful, it's gratitude that makes us joyful." Leaders who build a habit of gratitude, especially under pressure, create cultures where joy becomes more than a wishful thought. It becomes a source of fuel. Brené Brown's research confirms what I've experienced firsthand: Joy is not the absence of hardship, but the presence of something deeper. Her work shows that joy and resilience are interwoven. Joy isn't just a fleeting emotion; it's a spiritual practice. And when we nurture it, especially through daily gratitude, we build emotional reserves that carry us through life's challenges.

Gratitude is more than a mindset or feeling thankful; it's a daily practice that becomes a way of life. It's a powerful tool for regulation and resilience. It's a nervous system reset. When practiced consistently, it rewires our brains to look for what's right, even when so much feels wrong. When we intentionally practice gratitude, our brain releases dopamine and serotonin, two neurotransmitters that contribute to feelings of well-being and contentment.

Over time, this practice strengthens neural pathways that help us more easily access positive emotions quickly, even in times of stress. More importantly, gratitude activates the parasympathetic nervous system, the part of our autonomic nervous system responsible for rest, recovery, and restoration.

Remember, this system is the counterbalance to our stress response. When we are in a state of gratitude, we're not just thinking better, we're breathing slower, thinking clearer, and relating to others with more openness and authenticity. It gives us access to our calm brain and enables us to make good decisions and creatively problem solve.

I have had an intentional gratitude practice for much of my life, even before I realized what I was doing. I realized at an early age that feeling and expressing gratitude feels better and more helpful than hanging on to fear, frustration, and anger. I have practiced quickly switching to gratitude for so long that I often don't need to make the conscious choice to do it; it just is part of how I operate. It might be something simple and seemingly silly, like recognizing that I hit every green light or found a parking spot with ease, or something a bit deeper, like taking my dog for a walk every morning now that I am no longer tied to a corporate job and have more time.

In my coaching work, one of the most effective tools I've seen for building resilience is helping leaders reorient their internal dialogue toward gratitude. I have a client that I have been working with for some time who, over the last couple of years, has been intentional about his gratitude practice. We talk about this often, and I now see him not only expressing gratitude for his own life but also *expressing it to others*, often following up with me after our meetings to express his gratitude for my own words or presence. Recently, he shared an experience with me that made me pause. He had been training for months for his first Ironman race, involving hours of work, discomfort, and pushing both his body and his brain.

On average, it takes someone twelve to fourteen hours to complete the race, and he was doing incredibly well, hoping to finish and officially earn the coveted "Ironman" title. As he rounded the corner on foot, nearing the finish line, he passed his screaming family, cheering him on. Without warning, his three-year-old son ran to him, grabbed his hand, and together they crossed the finish line. His name was called, and his time was marked. Then, overwhelmed with gratitude for the experience and the touching moment of his son running alongside him, he heard the news: he was disqualified. His official record now read: *"No Finish Time"* and *"Disqualified: Finished with Child."* When he relayed the story to me, he sent a video of his son running with him and a picture of the disqualification notice. He called it *"very much worth it."*

I was so touched by his reaction. He could have easily gone to a place of frustration or sadness, upset by rules that—at least to me, as a non-Ironman human—feel a little silly. Honestly, I think he should have gotten extra credit for that finish. But instead, he immediately chose gratitude and joy: the satisfaction of knowing he finished, the sweetness of sharing the moment with his young son, and a story that will last a lifetime.

When we make the shift to lean into gratitude, we build resilience at both the neural and relational levels, shifting our focus from what's lacking to what's meaningful and working, broadening our perspective, activating our positive emotions, and strengthening our relationships. But it isn't just the feeling of gratitude that brings about these shifts; it is also the expression of it. Studies have shown that verbally acknowledging someone or writing a gratitude letter has a significantly stronger and longer-lasting impact than simply thinking grateful thoughts. Gratitude, like compassion, lives in action.

One of the most profound lessons I've learned about resilience came through personal experience during a season that cracked me open and showed me what it means to hold both grief and gratitude in the same breath. When my mom got sick, everything in my world shifted. Watching someone you love suffer is its own kind of heartbreak. The days were long, filled with unknowns, medical updates, and the quiet dread of impending loss. And yet, something surprising happened in the middle of that grief. I also started noticing moments of deep joy, like the warmth of her hand in mine, the way she smiled while I painted her nails or curled her hair, and the peace of sitting together in silence.

There were moments I would laugh and cry in the same hour, moments where gratitude for what we still had collided with sorrow for what we were losing. For a while, I thought that was wrong, like one emotion canceled out the other, but I've come to understand that real resilience is about learning to hold both.

Joy and grief, gratitude and grief, are both part of being fully alive. And it is this ability to feel deeply, to stay open, and to keep going that builds true resilience. Gratitude did not take away my grief. But it gave me ground to stand on. It gave me something to come back to.

That experience taught me this: resilience isn't about avoiding hard feelings. It's about expanding our capacity to feel the full spectrum, sorrow and hope, disappointment and joy. Gratitude helped me stay present, grounded, and connected. It helped regulate my nervous system and remind me that beauty can still exist in the middle of the mess. As I reflect, I continue to hold grief for the loss, gratitude for the lessons, and a commitment to pursuing joy with wholeheartedness.

So how does it all go together? Based on Brené Brown's research, there's a powerful emotional cycle at play: Gratitude fuels joy, joy builds resilience, and resilience sustains leadership, each step intentionally building the capacity for the next. Resilience is a crucial leadership muscle, and it's strengthened through the regular experience of joy. Not performative happiness or false positivity, but the kind of deep, quiet joy that's rooted in meaning, presence, and connection, and it starts with gratitude.

As we've discussed, gratitude takes intention, repetition, and a willingness to slow down and take notice. Here are a few of the tools I return to again and again, both personally and with my clients:

- Gratitude Lists: Start and end your day with three specific things you're grateful for.

- Spot the Simple Wins: Rewire your brain by celebrating everyday moments: a green light, a kind text, a great parking spot. The little things matter.

- Express It: Thank someone. Name what you appreciate about them. Send the email. Make the call. Speak it out loud.

- Believe Life is Happening For You: Even in difficulty, trust that there's something to be gained or grown.

The more you practice gratitude, the more resilient you become. Life doesn't become easier, but you become stronger, steadier, and more grounded within it.

Resilience isn't forged in comfort; it is shaped in the hard moments, when the stakes are high, the pressure is real, and the path isn't clear. In these moments, you don't have to be perfect; you just have to be present and choose to root yourself in rhythms and practices that regulate your nervous system, renew your energy, and restore your clarity.

Gratitude is one of the most powerful of those practices. It's free. It's accessible. And when practiced consistently, it begins to shift everything. When you lead from grounded resilience, your team will feel it. Through mirror neurons and the power of co-regulation, your internal state becomes a guidepost for those around you. When you breathe deeply, take pauses, and stay present under pressure, others will follow suit. You model a way of being that invites calm, clarity, and courage.

Gratitude fuels joy. Joy builds resilience. And resilience sustains leadership. This is not just a cycle, it's a strategy. It's how we lead well in the long run, stay human in the hard, and create cultures where others are empowered to do the same.

> **Reader Action:**
>
> 1. Think of a recent high-stress moment where dysregulation was present. How did you bounce back? How long did it take you to bounce back? What might have shifted if you had approached that high-stress moment with more intention around regulation?
>
> 2. Start a daily gratitude habit. For the next week, write down what you are grateful for: personally and professionally, big and small. When someone pops up in your gratitude list, reach out to them and express your gratitude directly through a coffee, a call, a text, or a note. At the end of the week, take note of how gratitude shifted your stress levels, mood, and interactions, and your ability to stay grounded in difficult moments.

CHAPTER 8

Leading and Identity

"Identity is not just what you do, it's who you are when everything else is stripped away."

In the high-stakes, high-pressure world of leadership, identity, or the way we understand, define, and express who we are to ourselves and to others, often becomes a quiet undercurrent. Our identity includes internal components such as our values, beliefs, personality, emotions, desires, and sense of purpose, and external components such as our roles, relationships, affiliations, achievements, and how we're perceived by others. In the context of leadership, identity is the compass that guides how we show up under pressure, make decisions, relate to others, and align with our values, regardless of titles or outcomes.

> IDENTITY IS NOT JUST WHAT YOU DO, IT'S **WHO YOU ARE** WHEN EVERYTHING ELSE IS STRIPPED AWAY.
>
> — SAM WILLING

Our identity shapes how we lead, how we respond under pressure, and how we define success. But too often, we tether our identity to things that can shift, break, or be taken from us: a job title, a board's approval, a company's performance, a salary, someone else's expectations. And when those things falter, as they inevitably do in leadership and in life, so does our sense of self. I've seen this countless times in my career, leaders attaching their identity to what they do and anchoring it to a specific outcome that they believe will equate to success in the world. But we are so much more than what we do. We are layered and unique beings with unique values and a unique purpose.

When we begin to operate in a way that honors our uniqueness and reclaim the parts of us that we quieted in the name of success, we unlock something profound. We become anchored in what lasts, which keeps us steady no matter what storms come.

Within the field of biotech, where I have spent a significant portion of my career, lie some of the highest failure rates in the business world. Sixty percent of startups fail within the first five years, and ninety percent fail before achieving meaningful success such as an IPO, acquisition, or fully approved product.

These are some of the highest failure rates in the business world. The odds of getting a drug to market are only around ten percent, and doing it before you run out of time and money is almost impossible. So when I work with biotech executives who have tied their identity to their company's trajectory in one of the riskiest industries, I get worried. The risks are high and the stakes are personal, as many of them genuinely want to make a difference for the patients they serve, but also want to reach a level of personal success that makes all of the hard work and sacrifice seem "worth it".

I once coached a struggling CEO who had wrapped his entire identity around his title and the success of a drug reaching the market. And when the company ran out of time and money, his self-worth, confidence, and leadership crumbled with it, which was noticed and felt by everyone around him. He wasn't just grieving a failed company, but a piece of himself. The failure deeply impacted him, and so did the disorientation of not knowing who he was outside of the company, without the status or the mission.

I have experienced this grief myself. When I left my executive role at the time to care for my mom, I grieved hard. I had helped build the company from scratch, paying special attention to the culture and the people. I was respected, I had a seat at the strategic table, and when I walked away from all of it, I was humbled and disappointed to realize how much of my identity was tied up in my title, my responsibilities, and my salary.

The anecdote to this identity crisis begins by exploring self-awareness, specifically, whether the beliefs your identity is rooted in are lasting, true, and self-defined. Once you understand this, you can start to rebuild your identity around who you *really* are. Identity is something we can construct; we have agency in shaping it. The heart of authentic leadership is congruency, or living and leading from a place of alignment and truth rather than external factors. When we do the internal work around our identity and become congruent, we can align our behaviors, and when we align our behaviors, our internal identity radiates outward, having a profound impact on others around us. When our head, heart, and hands are connected, we foster authenticity and build trust.

When I work with leaders on reconnecting with their true identity, one of the things we focus on is legacy, and I challenge them to think deeply about the impact they want to leave. Leadership isn't just about a moment in time, a role, or a season; it is about the mark we leave on others. We have a limited amount of time to do so: one set of hands, one pair of feet, one brain, one smile, and when we are gone, the only thing that will remain is our legacy.

"Legacy" is defined as "the long-lasting impact of particular events or actions that took place in the past or of a person's life." I thought about this a lot when my mom passed. I thought about the legacy she left, the legacy I wanted to leave, and whether or not my current priorities and actions were in alignment with that legacy. In some areas, they were, but in others, they were not. After I was laid off, I had space and time to do some of my own work around legacy and identity, and as part of the work, I dove into the beliefs and labels I had attached to myself over the years. I thought about who I was and who I wanted to be. I analyzed what I had always considered to be truths about myself. I checked in with myself on my core values and asked myself some hard questions about where I was incongruent, and I realized that I had compartmentalized so much of my life.

At work, I was what I now call "Corporate Sam," and everywhere else, I was the rest of me. While some traits were congruent in both of those identities, there were also incongruent ways that I lived in both worlds, masking and protecting myself.

"Identity Regulation Theory" describes the tension between our internal and external identity, in other words, who we are versus who we think we are expected to be. When there is a gap between the internal and external identities, we often manage it by hiding parts of ourselves. Eventually, the hiding and compartmentalizing take a toll and lead us into feelings of inauthenticity and burnout as we try to maintain both our external persona and manage our internal feelings. While this is often about self-protection and preservation, it often disconnects us from others, painting false images of ourselves for others. This flies in the face of what we know, which is that people follow authenticity, not perfection.

When it comes to identity, particularly in a work environment, women face some additional challenges. Let's face it, women have struggled to receive fair and equitable treatment and opportunities forever. While this book isn't about that, it is an issue close to my heart that I feel I must touch on. If you are a woman reading this, I hope you feel seen. If you are a man and reading this, I hope it gives you pause for reflection.

Most women learn from an early age that in order to have opportunities, be taken seriously, and succeed, we need to show up in a certain way. We've been taught to overperform, under-emote, and edit ourselves. We've grown our careers being extra intentional about the clothes we wear, our body language, facial expressions, and how much we talk about our personal lives, especially our children and our pregnancies, and carrying what has been termed "invisible work" at home and in the workplace. We push aside important leadership traits like compassion, empathy, and intuition in order to have a seat at the table.

All the while, we are paid less, have different standards for promotions, have been penalized for having babies, and have been chastised for the unexpected ways we are depended upon, like caring for sick children, aging parents, and taking care of home responsibilities. This cycle leads many of us into burnout, operating from a split identity instead of wholeness. But living and leading split means the world misses out on so much magic. There is incredible power when a woman combines intuition, emotional resilience, and compassion with tangible strategy and skills.

Over the years, many women have been referred to me by their organizations to work on their leadership behaviors after being labeled "too emotional," "too aggressive," or even of "having sharp elbows." Most of the time, I end up coaching these women on how to navigate the environments they are in, helping them recognize that their behaviors are not too emotional or aggressive but assertive. We work on setting boundaries, clarifying expectations, leading well, and being taken seriously.

Their male counterparts are allowed and encouraged to show up equally or more aggressively, using foul language, raising their voices, and crassly joking, and they're received with nodding heads and chuckles.

I will never forget working in an HR manager role when my children were young. My boss at the time was a traditionalist. There was no such thing as remote work or flexibility, and I was expected to be in the office from 8 a.m. to 5 p.m., five days a week. In fact, he often did what he called a "walk around" a few minutes before 5 p.m. most evenings, cataloging who was still at their desks and who had left a few minutes early.

Fortunately, I always took my jobs seriously, and this one was no exception. The only problem was that I had young children, and I failed to recognize a really important reality. We only have one hundred percent to give, no more and no less, for all areas of our lives. And in that job, I spent the hours between 7:30 a.m. and 5:30 p.m. every day pretending I didn't have children and then white-knuckled it home every night to give what was left to them.

One day, I was at work and got the dreaded call from the school…one of my children had lice. With my husband out of town, I raced home to pick my child up from school and immediately bought all of the supplies for treatment. When we arrived home, I checked my other child and myself, and as it turned out, we had lice, too. If you have never experienced this, consider yourself lucky. When lice sweep through a home, it is a full-time job. It's showers with special shampoo. It's combing endlessly. It's washing clothes, bedding, and pillows, not to mention the grossness of it all. To do it all, I had to take a day off, which I relayed to my boss as a family emergency. When I returned to work the next day and gave him a glimpse of the last twenty-four hours, he looked at me, like an alien, and said, "I never had to deal with any of that. My wife stayed home." And just like that, it was back to business. I felt so alone.

A few months later, I left that job with the intention of taking a break and pursuing roles that offered more flexibility and allowed me to be more present at home. When I gave my notice, my boss cautioned me "Sam, you are talented and you could go far at this company, if you leave now, you may never be able to get back into the workforce, you will lose credibility by having a gap in your resume" I cried all the way home, I loved working, and I loved being a mom and I wanted to do it all with excellence but I needed to do it in a way that aligned with my values and one of those values was being present for my children.

A few weeks after I left, I got my first coaching client and then landed a job with more flexibility working for an inspiring female leader. Before I said yes to the role, I set a boundary I had never set before: I said that I needed to leave the office by 3:00 p.m. each day so that, as long as I had children at home, I would be there when they got home from school.

For the rest of my corporate career, that became my non-negotiable boundary. Because of that commitment and aligning my actions with said value, I was able to be present with my children, and operate with high performance, and my career grew as a result.

If we are going to lead from a place of wholeness, we need to recognize where we have stowed parts of ourselves away in order to conform. I have witnessed firsthand the power of leaders stepping into wholeness and the impact of doing so on others.

The story in Chapter 5 about the CEO who hid her cancer diagnosis out of fear that it would make others perceive her as incapable is a perfect example of this. When she finally made the decision to be vulnerable with her organization, the barriers that had been present came down, and trust was restored. She led with her humanity, and as a result, led others to do the same. It was a beautiful thing to bear witness to.

To this day, she is the most authentic CEO I have ever worked with, but it's cost her time, money, and energy. The work isn't easy, but there is an ease that comes from operating as her authentic self.

As you begin to explore what it means to lead from your true identity, here are a few powerful practices I use with leaders to help bring clarity, alignment, and confidence. These practices offer a starting point, glimpses into the deeper, transformational work of becoming a more grounded and authentic leader. If something here stirs something in you, that's your invitation. This work is most impactful when done with the guidance of a coach who can help you uncover what's true, shed what no longer fits, and lead from the inside out.

- **Defining Core Values:** Your core values are the anchor of your identity. They are the steady truths that remain when titles fade, seasons shift, and pressure rises. Knowing your core values allows you to respond with clarity rather than react out of fear or confusion. When I work with clients, we identify their top values and then explore where their behaviors align and where they don't. This awareness becomes a compass. Want to lead with authenticity and resilience? Start by asking: *What do I stand for when no one is watching?*

- **Creating I AM Statements:** "I AM" statements are powerful declarations of identity that reframe the stories we tell ourselves. These are not about roles or achievements, but about character, calling, and truth. Leaders often say, "I'm just someone who pushes through," or "I'm the one who always has to have the answers." But what if you rewrote that to say, "I am a grounded leader who leads with compassion and courage"? When we reframe identity from within, we begin to live and lead from that place. I help leaders name and embody these truths so they show up with intention and impact.

- **Defining Your Legacy:** Legacy isn't just what you leave behind when you're gone; it's what people experience in your presence. It's the mark your leadership leaves on hearts, not just business outcomes. In coaching, we explore this question: What do you want others to say changed because they knew you or worked with you? Thinking in terms of legacy helps you move from urgency to intentionality and reframes success from short-term wins to long-term impact, realigning how leaders spend their time, energy, and focus.

- **Feedback and Coaching:** We all have blind spots, ways of operating we can't fully see because we're inside our own story. That's where coaching and meaningful feedback come in. Feedback, when rooted in trust, is a mirror, not a judgment. In our work together, I help leaders receive and process feedback with curiosity instead of defensiveness. Together, we uncover identity narratives that no longer serve you and strengthen the ones that do. Coaching provides a safe place to rewire not just what you do but how you see yourself, and that changes everything.

In a world that often rewards performance over presence and output over authenticity, it can be tempting to focus all of your energy on the external markers of success like metrics, milestones, influence, and achievement. But the most impactful leaders I know have done the deep, sometimes uncomfortable, inner work of getting clear on who they are beyond the titles, beyond the expectations, and beyond the noise.

Identity isn't what you do. It's who you are when no one is watching. It's the core that remains steady when circumstances shift, when roles end, or when success doesn't come as planned. If you skip the inner work, you risk building a version of leadership that may be admirable but isn't sustainable. Alignment is the key, not just with your values, but with your way of being in the world.

When you are anchored in your true identity, you lead differently. You lead with clarity, confidence, and care. You respond instead of react. You create psychological safety because people feel your presence is grounded, not performative.

Fear-based leadership driven by scarcity, protection, and force may achieve short-term results but often costs trust, connection, and joy. Freedom-based leadership, on the other hand, is expansive and grounded in trust, authenticity, and the willingness to surrender the illusion of control in exchange for something much greater: meaningful impact that lasts.

Consider this your invitation. Come back to yourself. Do the work. Reclaim the pieces of your identity you've quieted to conform or achieve. Align your behaviors with your deepest values. And lead in a way that not only feels true but inspires others to do the same.

When you know who you are, you don't just lead *well*. You lead *whole*.

Reader Action:

1. What parts of your identity are currently tied to things you could lose? If they were stripped away, what would remain? What values, truths, or qualities define who you are at your core, regardless of circumstances?

2. Ask yourself the question: *What is the impact I want to make on others in my life and in my work?* and reflect on what needs to shift in how you're currently showing up to align more fully with that impact. Are your daily actions reinforcing the legacy you want to leave, or are they pulling you away from it?

CHAPTER 9

Integration and Alignment

BEFORE WE EXPLORE specific tools and practices for nervous system regulation, I want to talk about how to approach this work with grace, patience, and intention.

This is not about getting it perfect. It's not about mastering a checklist of calming behaviors. It's about learning to return to yourself, again and again.

Regulation is not a one-time achievement. It's a lifelong practice. There is no finish line where you'll say, "I've arrived. I never get triggered anymore." That's not the goal. That's not even realistic.

You will be triggered. We live in a fast, demanding world, and we are fully human. So the goal isn't to eliminate dysregulation but to *recognize* it and to feel the physiological shift in your body and then choose to meet it with tools that bring you back to center.

That's the heart of this chapter: learning how to notice when you're moving out of alignment and then how to return.

Many of my clients come into this work craving immediate results. They want a protocol, a plan, a perfect morning routine. And while I love a good routine, I always remind them that integration isn't a sprint but a slow layering in. If you try to add everything at once, you'll likely feel more stressed, not less.

This work invites a shift in posture: from urgency to curiosity, from performance to presence.

Choose one or two tools to begin. Stick with them. Notice what actually moves your body from activation to calm. Some practices might feel awkward at first. Others might surprise you with their simplicity. But with repetition, they'll become second nature in anchoring you in the chaos.

And as you begin to follow through on these practices, you'll build something even more powerful than calm: You'll build trust in yourself. You'll become someone who keeps promises to yourself and someone who leads from steadiness, not just strength.

That's what this chapter offers: not a path to perfection, but a way back to yourself.

Let's begin.

Regulation Tools and Practices

1. Breathwork

When life gets loud, breathwork brings us home to ourselves. Just five minutes of intentional breathing each day can dramatically reduce anxiety and increase positive emotions. Intentional breathwork doesn't just calm us, it changes us. Breathing influences the interoceptive processes responsible for self-awareness, emotional regulation, and decision-making. By regulating your breath, you are literally reshaping how your brain and body respond to stress.

Below are three powerful tools simple enough to do anywhere, even in the boardroom. If done with intention, these exercises will shift your state in just a few minutes.

- **Box Breathing**

    This technique, developed by former Navy SEAL Mark Divine, is a tool designed to help you regain control of your nervous system, especially during high-stress moments. Box breathing activates the parasympathetic nervous system, signaling your body it's safe to rest, digest, and recover. It's especially helpful before a meeting or presentation, or after receiving difficult news.

Instructions:

1. Breathe out slowly, emptying your lungs completely.
2. Breathe in through your nose for a count of four.
3. Hold your breath for a count of four.
4. Exhale slowly through your mouth for a count of four.
5. Hold your breath again for a count of four.
6. Repeat three to four rounds.

- **Diaphragmatic Breathing**

Also called "belly breathing," this practice draws air deep into your lungs and engages your diaphragm, a powerful signal to your body that it's safe to slow down. Research by Hopper et al. (2019) found that diaphragmatic breathing lowers respiratory rate, cortisol levels, and blood pressure, making it a powerful tool for both physical and emotional regulation.

Instructions:

1. Sit or lie comfortably and place one hand on your belly and one on your chest.
2. Inhale deeply through your nose, letting your belly rise (not your chest).
3. Exhale slowly through your mouth, letting your belly fall.
4. Repeat for five to ten breaths, allowing your body to relax more with each round.

2. 5 Senses Grounding (5-4-3-2-1)

This practice helps anchor you in the present moment by engaging your senses. It's especially effective during moments of panic, overwhelm, or mental spiraling and can be done out loud or in your mind. By focusing on what's around you, you gently shift your attention away from worry and into your body.

Instructions:

1. Name 5 things you can see.
2. Name 4 things you can touch.
3. Name 3 things you can hear.
4. Name 2 things you can smell.
5. Name 1 thing you can taste.

This practice is both grounding and calming, like putting your emotional feet back on solid ground.

3. Meditation

If breathwork is the door, meditation is the quiet room behind it. Both regulate the nervous system, but meditation invites us to linger longer in the space between stimulus and response. It's where we practice stillness, deepen awareness, and gently retrain our brains toward calm and clarity.

Using breath and mindfulness, meditation activates the parasympathetic nervous system, slowing heart rate, lowering blood pressure, and reducing emotional reactivity. Over time, it doesn't just help you feel better, but helps you live and lead better.

Research from UC Davis Health and other institutions has shown that consistent meditation practice leads to:

- Reduced stress and anxiety
- Improved memory, attention, and sleep

- Enhanced willpower and emotional regulation
- Greater compassion toward self and others
- Decreased pain and blood pressure

Many leaders find success with guided meditations through apps like Headspace, Insight Timer, or Calm, but even a few minutes of silence each day can create a profound shift.

How to Practice Meditation:

1. Find a quiet space where you can sit comfortably with your eyes closed.
2. Connect with your body, rest your hands gently, relax your shoulders, and notice any tension.
3. Begin deep breathing, using a pattern like box breathing or simply inhaling slowly through your nose and exhaling through your mouth.
4. Notice where your thoughts go. It's normal for your mind to wander. Gently bring your attention back to your breath.
5. End with a simple affirmation like, "I am grounded," or "I am safe and calm."

Start with just three to five minutes. Over time, the stillness will stretch.

4. Journaling

When your thoughts are spinning or emotions feel heavy, journaling helps create space. Research shows that writing by hand can activate your parasympathetic nervous system, the one responsible for calming and grounding you. It slows you down, clarifies your thinking, and helps you reconnect with your internal compass.

This isn't about writing perfectly or even every day. It's about presence and honesty. When you put pen to paper, you regulate from the inside out. If you're in a state of overwhelm or feel dysregulated, try a brain dump. Write down everything in your head: no punctuation, no structure, no filter. Then take a deep breath. You've just made room for clarity.

How to Start:

1. Choose a quiet space.
   Somewhere you feel safe, unrushed, and uninterrupted, even for just five minutes. For most people, journaling first thing in the morning or at the end of the day works best.

2. Use a physical notebook or journal.
   Handwriting slows the mind and deepens emotional processing.

3. Pick one prompt or simply free-write.
   Let your thoughts flow without censoring or judging.

Simple Journal Prompts to Regulate:

- What am I feeling right now, physically, emotionally, and spiritually?
- What do I need today?
- What am I grateful for?
- What's one thing I want to let go of?
- What's one thing I want to hold onto?
- What's draining me? What's energizing me?
- What good thing might happen today?
- I am a person who...

5. Visualization

Visualization is a powerful tool that guides your nervous system into a regulated state by allowing you to picture peace, safety, or success. Just a few minutes of intentional imagery can reduce stress, calm anxiety, and even interrupt destructive thought loops.

It's not about escaping reality; it's about rehearsing resilience, positivity, and your desired outcome and directing your energy with intention. I often use this technique before intense meetings, challenging conversations, or public speaking by visualizing the version of myself who is grounded and steady under pressure before stepping into her shoes and letting her lead.

How To Start:

1. Find a quiet space.
   Sit or lie down comfortably with minimal distractions.

2. Close your eyes and breathe deeply.
   Use a breathing technique like box breathing or deep inhales and slow exhales.

3. Picture something that brings you peace or a positive outcome you desire.
   A serene place. A moment of confidence. A future version of yourself, grounded and calm.

Visualization Tips:

- Be consistent. Start with three to five minutes daily or when under pressure. This primes your brain in powerful ways.

- Personalize it. Picture your calm place, whether it's a mountaintop, a cozy room, or your child's laughter.

- Engage the senses. What can you see, hear, smell, touch, or taste in that scene?

- Pair it with breathwork or journaling for deeper grounding.

- Journal afterward. Reflect on how you felt and what your body or spirit needed most.

6. I AM Statements

When you're under pressure, your nervous system tends to default to old scripts: *I'm not enough, I can't handle this, or I'm failing.* Practicing I AM statements is a powerful form of self-compassion that rewires those narratives with truth and kindness by speaking directly to your identity, not your output, and anchoring you in who you really are through your values, not your circumstances.

The act of creating I AM statements and building them into your daily practice increases resilience and builds self-trust by reinforcing your true identity and reminding yourself who you are when life feels shaky.

How To Create and Use I AM Statements:

1. Identify your core values and define how a person living in alignment with those values shows up.

2. Create I AM statements for that version of yourself and write them down. I AM statements focus on who you are becoming, not just what you're doing.

3. Every day, take a few moments to ground yourself. Take a few breaths. Notice if you're being hard on yourself or spinning in negative self-talk.

4. Speak or write your I AM statements. Keep them in front of you. Refer to them often.

Examples:
- I am a calm and grounded leader, even when things are uncertain.
- I am learning. I am growing. I don't need to have it all figured out today.
- I am enough, exactly as I am.
- I am a person who follows through on what matters most.
- I am a compassionate leader to others and myself.

7. Bilateral Stimulation and Movement

Emotions aren't just in your head; they live in your body. That's why movement, especially bilateral stimulation, the act of activating both sides of the body in a rhythmic, alternating way, is such a powerful tool for nervous system regulation.

Whether it's walking, tapping, or dancing, these gentle, repetitive movements engage both hemispheres of the brain and help reduce anxiety, improve focus, and restore calm. When you are moving in this way, you are stimulating both sides of your brain, which restores cognitive balance and clarity, and increases endorphins, your body's natural mood boosters.

A study by Sakuragi & Sugiyama (2006) found that daily walking improved participants' affect and their ability to regulate the parasympathetic nervous system. More recent research (Guo et al., 2023) supports the use of bilateral stimulation to enhance executive functioning, helping people stay clear, accurate, and focused, especially under stress.

I recommend using bilateral movement daily as a grounding ritual, even if just for five minutes. Try it before or after tough meetings, transitions, or emotional conversations, and pair it with breathwork or an I AM statement to maximize calm and clarity.

How To Practice Bilateral Stimulation:

You don't need fancy equipment, just your body. Try one of these anytime you feel overwhelmed, distracted, or ungrounded:

1. Walking
   Take a short walk, indoors or outdoors. Let your arms swing gently. As you walk, notice the alternating rhythm: left foot, right foot. Breathe deeply.

2. Tapping
   - Gently tap your left shoulder with your right hand, then your right shoulder with your left hand. Alternate rhythmically.

- Do the same with your knees or heels.
- Use a slow, steady tempo (about one tap per second) and continue for one to two minutes.

3. Cross-Body Movement
   - March in place and touch your right hand to your left knee, then your left hand to your right knee.
   - Or try a gentle cross-body stretch, reaching one arm across to the opposite side and alternating.

8. Nature

Sometimes the best regulation tool doesn't come from a screen, a strategy, or a structured practice. It comes from stepping outside.

Spending time in nature is one of the most powerful and most accessible ways to activate your parasympathetic nervous system, or, as you learned earlier, your body's rest-and-digest state. Research consistently shows that being in natural environments lowers cortisol, reduces blood pressure, and eases tension in both the body and the mind.

Whether it's five minutes in the sun or a walk through a tree-lined path, nature is a cost-free, calming tool for nervous system regulation. I encourage all of my clients to build nature into their daily routine, and when paired with breathwork, journaling, and I AM statements. It is a powerful way to take a purposeful pause.

How To Use Nature to Regulate:

You don't have to go off the grid; just go outside with intention:

1. Sunlight Reset: Step outside and turn your face toward the sun. Close your eyes and take a few slow breaths. Let yourself be still for a few minutes, noticing the warmth, light, and air around you.

2. Forest or Tree-Lined Walk: Take a short walk near trees, plants, or water. If possible, walk without earbuds or distractions. Listen to the natural sounds and match your breath to your footsteps.

3. Barefoot Grounding: Stand barefoot on grass, dirt, or sand. Feel the sensations under your feet. This kind of grounding, also known as "earthing," helps calm your nervous system and reconnects you with your body.

4. Sit Spot: Find a "sit spot" outside (a bench, a rock, or a blanket on the grass) where you can just be. Let your senses guide you. What do you see, hear, smell, and feel?

9. Human Connection & Co-Regulation

Sometimes, the most powerful way to calm your nervous system is not something you do alone, but something you share. In fact, humans are biologically wired for connection. When we feel seen, safe, and supported by someone else, our nervous system often begins to calm, even if nothing else has changed.

This is called "co-regulation," and it's one of the most effective, underused regulatory tools we have. Through the science of mirror neurons, we now know that emotional states are contagious. When you're near someone grounded, your body begins to match their rhythm. When we are with someone we trust, our amygdala, or our fear center, calms down. I encourage my clients to identify their "regulation people" who feel safe, steady, and nonjudgmental. Once you find your regulation people, practice connecting and reaching out before you're overwhelmed. Pay attention to those around you for whom you can serve as a co-regulator, and model the calm and compassion you want to pass on.

How to Co-Regulate:

You can practice co-regulation both as the one receiving support and as the one offering it.

1. Sit with someone safe. Being in the physical presence of a calm, compassionate person can shift your entire physiology. You don't need to talk; just being together matters.

2. Make eye contact: Gentle, safe eye contact is a subtle but powerful way to foster connection and invite calm.

3. Name what's happening: Whether for yourself or someone else, naming the emotion activates self-awareness and signals safety to the brain.

4. Use a grounded voice: Lowering your tone and slowing your speech can help signal regulation, both to others and to your own body.

5. Offer or receive a hug: Physical touch, when safe and welcomed, releases oxytocin and slows the nervous system's stress response.

10. Smiling

It may seem too simple to be powerful, but smiling is one of the easiest and most effective ways to send calming signals to your nervous system. When you smile (even a fake one!), your body responds with a cascade of chemical and physiological changes that move you toward a more regulated, grounded state.

This is more than just a mood boost; it's biological regulation in action. Smiling releases dopamine, serotonin, and endorphins, which are neurochemicals that reduce stress, boost mood, and even relieve pain, triggering your parasympathetic nervous system and helping your body shift into rest-and-recover mode. Smiling is also relational, as it creates an unspoken invitation to connect. It's an outward expression of regulation that can help others regulate, too. Your smile is more than an expression; it's a regulatory tool, a connection signal, and a reminder that calm and compassion are always available.

You don't have to wait to feel joyful to smile.
Sometimes the smile comes first and the calm follows.

How to use smiling for regulation:

1. Practice smiling during stress: Try softening your expression when you feel tension rising. Even a subtle smile can send a calming signal inward.

2. Smile at someone else: Passing on a smile activates mirror neurons in others, triggering their own regulatory response and reinforcing yours.

3. Pair it with breath: Inhale slowly, then exhale while smiling gently. This pairs two regulatory tools in one and signals calm throughout your system.

4. Smile in the mirror: This might feel silly, but it's powerful. Offering yourself a kind, compassionate smile in the mirror is a form of self-regulation.

Additional Practices I Have Found Helpful in My Regulation Journey

These next tools are ones I return to again and again, not just in my own life, but in nearly every coaching conversation I have. They help identify what drains your energy, what restores it, and how to steward it with greater intention and clarity.

I use these myself, and they've become foundational in how I guide my clients through the work of regulation and alignment. These practices offer practical insight into your day-to-day rhythms, and they gently invite you to make more life-giving choices, both personally and professionally.

Drains and Gains:

Let's talk about how you spend your energy, because how you manage your energy is just as important as how you manage your time.

I want you to start noticing what gives you energy and what drains it. Think about everything: work activities, personal tasks, conversations, and even certain people. Make two lists: one for your gains (the things that leave you feeling filled up, centered, or inspired) and one for your drains (the things that deplete you, make you tense, or leave you feeling scattered). I kept track of mine for over a month to ensure I captured most activities.

Once you've got your list, here's the important part:

- Prioritize your gains. These are your lifelines. Put more of your time and energy into them, even if it's just small, consistent doses.

- Set boundaries around your drains. That might mean saying no, delegating, or limiting time with people who consistently pull you out of alignment. It's okay to protect your peace.

- And for the drains you can't avoid? Build in recovery time. That might mean a short walk after a tough meeting, ten minutes of quiet after school drop-off, or a calming ritual before bed. Your nervous system needs time to reset.

You don't have to overhaul everything at once. Just begin by getting honest about what fills you and what empties you, and start making decisions with that awareness at the center.

Start/Keep/Stop:

This is a simple reflection tool to help you identify what habits or mindsets you want to start, continue, or release. It helps bring awareness to patterns that are either nourishing or eroding your regulation.

This is one of my favorite reflection tools because it's simple, honest, and powerful. It's about getting clear on how you're using your energy and making intentional commitments to yourself about where it's going next.

Take a moment and reflect on the rhythms of your life and leadership. Then ask yourself three questions:

- *What do I want to start doing?*
  What new habit, practice, or mindset would support me right now? What's something I know would help me feel more grounded, alive, or aligned, even if it's small?

- *What do I want to keep doing?*
  What's already working well for me? What do I want to protect, repeat, or give more space to in my life?

- *What do I want to stop doing?*
  What's no longer serving me? It might be a behavior, a belief, a habit, or even a way I've been speaking to myself. Where am I leaking energy?

This isn't about adding pressure or trying to perfect your life. It's about honoring what you need and taking just one or two steps in the direction of greater alignment. When you make intentional shifts, especially small ones, you begin to build deeper trust in yourself.

Remember: You don't have to do everything at once. But you do get to choose how you show up. This list helps you do that with clarity and compassion.

Managing Your Inputs:

Let's slow down for a moment and take an honest, compassionate look at what you're consuming, not just food but everything you're letting into your body, mind, and spirit.

When you're under stress, it's easy to reach for what feels like relief in the moment: an extra cup of caffeine, sugary snacks, or one more glass of wine to unwind. And let's be honest, sometimes these things do help us feel better for a minute. But often, they're not true regulation, but *medication*. They bypass your deeper needs and keep us running on fumes.

I'm not here to judge your inputs, but I do want to invite you to notice them.

Ask yourself:

- *What am I reaching for when I feel anxious, drained, or overwhelmed?*
- *Do my inputs nourish and stabilize me or spike and crash me?*
- *Am I consuming out of intention or out of habit?*

Start to pay attention to what you're putting into your system, from food and drink to music and television, including the tone of your own self-talk. Inputs are powerful.

They either bring you closer to your grounded, regulated self, or they pull you further away.

It's about awareness, compassion, and moving with intention. When you notice what's not working, you can start choosing what does.

And if you do find yourself reaching for a quick fix like we all do, pause and ask:

What do I really need right now?
Then, choose something that helps you return, not escape.

You deserve nourishment, not noise.

Wheel of Life:

Sometimes, we get so focused on one part of life, whether it's our work, our leadership, or a challenge we're facing, that we lose sight of the whole. The "Wheel of Life" is a powerful snapshot that helps you zoom out and take stock, and offers a clear picture of where you're thriving and where things may feel off.

Look across key areas like:

- Work & Purpose
- Health & Energy
- Relationships & Connection
- Spirituality & Faith
- Rest & Play
- Growth & Development
- Finances

This is about gently noticing where your energy is going and where it might need to be redirected. Often, we pour into one area while unintentionally neglecting another. This tool helps you bring that into awareness and begin to rebalance.

As you reflect, ask yourself:

What's one area I've been neglecting that actually matters deeply to me?
Use that insight to guide where you might direct more energy or develop a new practice.

Recognizing The Pressure You're In:

Before we talk about adding anything new, like habits, routines, or practices, let's stop and name the reality you're living in.

Are you...

- Navigating layoffs or organizational stress?
- Making tough decisions that impact people you care about?
- Short on sleep, movement, or meaningful nourishment?
- Overstimulated by news, meetings, notifications, or demands at home?

This isn't just life; it's pressure. And it matters.

When you're in a season like this, the most powerful thing you can do is acknowledge it with compassion. It's not the time to pile on goals or beat yourself up for not "doing more." It's the time to slow down, choose one small thing that helps you feel more like yourself, and create pockets of recovery.

Integration doesn't begin with hustle. It begins with honesty and grace. Ask yourself: *Given what I'm carrying, what would support and not stretch me right now?*

That's the work. Gentle, wise, sustainable.

Micro-Recoveries:

Let's be honest. Some days don't allow for a long walk, a full journal entry, or a deep breathwork session between back-to-back meetings or family responsibilities. That's where micro-recoveries come in.

These are tiny, intentional one- to three-minute pauses you build into your day. A moment to step outside. A slow breath with your hand on your heart. A stretch between meetings. A genuine smile at someone you love or even just at yourself.

Think of micro-recoveries as nervous system pit stops: small, simple resets that help bring you back into your body and recenter your energy.

They don't require you to change your schedule. They just ask you to show up and remind your nervous system: *You're safe. You're steady. You've got this.*

Try sprinkling a few throughout your day:

- Between meetings
- After a difficult conversation
- When transitioning from work to home
- Right before sleep

Over time, these micro-moments build a deep reserve of resilience and remind you that regulation doesn't always require a big block of time; it just requires presence.

Spiritual and Inner Anchoring:

Sometimes the most powerful regulation comes not from doing, but from remembering. Remembering that we are not alone, that there is something greater holding us.

For me, that anchor is God. My faith is a lifeline. I believe that God is love, and that love is constant, steady, and available to me at all times. It's what grounds me when everything else feels like it's shifting.

Your spiritual anchor may look different. For some, it's prayer. For others, it's nature, silence, music, or simply the feeling of being part of something bigger. Faith, however you define it, is not about perfection. It's about presence. It's a space to return to when the world feels heavy, and a reminder that regulation isn't just internal, but it's also about where we root ourselves.

Be curious:

- *What brings you peace?*
- *What reminds you that you're connected?*
- *What helps you release control and feel held?*

As we close this chapter, I want to remind you that you don't need to do everything at once. If you choose just three things to begin integrating, I recommend movement without stressful inputs, box breathing, and journaling by writing a short gratitude list each day. Start small, stay consistent, and let the work meet you where you are.

Healing is about returning to who you've always been. When we live from alignment, it changes everything: our leadership, our relationships, our self-talk. Regulated leadership doesn't mean being calm all the time, but coming back every time. That return is where your power lives.

Regulation is a daily choice. And it's one that builds identity and integrity over time, through steady, aligned practices. You don't need more action. You need more awareness. Think of regulation as the "exhale" that makes sustained performance possible.

The next time you're in a meeting and feel your body shift into a stress state, pause. Breathe. Grab a notepad and doodle. Write a grounding word. Try a silent mantra. Step outside if you can. Box breathe through your nose. In just ninety seconds, you can come back to yourself. And every time you do, you build trust. With your body. With your mind. With your life.

Reader Action:

1. What is one area of your life or leadership that you feel tension around and would like to shift? How can you meet that tension with self-compassion instead of judgment? What would progress look like for you right now?

2. Choose one regulation practice to commit to daily for one week. Track how you feel before and after. Notice where you are gaining clarity, energy, and peace.

Conclusion

AT ITS HEART, this book has been about one thing: learning to lead from a place of wholeness, where your head, heart, and body are aligned. Regulated leadership isn't about being calm all the time. It's about knowing how to return, again and again, to presence, to clarity, and to the truth of who you are when everything else is stripped away.

Thank you for walking with me through these pages. For choosing to slow down, reflect, and explore what it really means to lead with intention, courage, and compassion. I know your time is sacred, and I don't take it lightly that you spent some of it here.

My deepest hope is that you leave this book feeling more rooted in who you are and more equipped to lead in a way that honors your identity, your values, your vision, and your nervous system. I hope that you've felt seen, challenged, and encouraged not to strive for perfection, but to lead with presence and excellence. To trust that the real transformation doesn't come from fixing, but from returning to yourself. Not from more action, but from more awareness and self-compassion.

Healing isn't about becoming someone new. It's about returning to who you've always been. And that version of you, the regulated, grounded, and authentic version, is the leader the world needs.

And let me be clear, you *are* a leader. No matter your title, your role, or where you find yourself today, you have places and circles in your life where you hold influence. You have agency. And that means you have a choice every day about how you show up and interact with the world. Others may hold different titles or wield different decision-making powers, but beneath it all, we are all human beings. What makes you special isn't your salary, your position, or your achievements; it's that you are uniquely made, and there is a distinct calling on your life that no one else can fulfill.

A year ago, I traveled to Mexico with my dad and sister to scatter my mom's ashes. We were on a boat. My sister gently removed the ashes from the urn and placed them on the deck. I was so struck at that moment by what was left of my mom, her physical form reduced to ash. Ultimately, I know her spirit and legacy live on, but in that moment, I was overwhelmed with the reality that we have a limited amount of time to walk this earth.

How we use this time matters. And who we impact matters the most.

I will not waste another moment holding myself back in work, in relationships, or in life, and I don't want you to, either. If you are willing to surrender, to enter into the self-discovery work, and if you show up with openness and willingness, I promise you that it will be the most beautiful unfolding. It will bring ease, alignment, and strength to boldly and calmly step forward in your true identity.

You've done brave work by reading this far. Now, the invitation is to continue practicing with intention and action.

If you're ready to step more fully into your regulated leadership, I'd be honored to walk alongside you. Whether you're an executive seeking personal transformation, a founder navigating complexity, or a company committed to building a more human, high-performing culture, this work is for you.

Through executive coaching, leadership cohorts, culture consulting, and retreats, I help leaders and organizations move from burnout and breakdown to clarity, confidence, and sustainable impact. Because when a leader learns to regulate, everything changes, from decision-making and team dynamics to trust, resilience, and results.

This is more than theory. It's practice. It's transformation. It's the hidden key to powerful leadership and personal peace.

Scan the QR code below to access free tools referenced in this book, including the *Wheel of Life* and *Self-Compassion Practice Guide*, and explore how we can work together to equip you and your team for what's next.

Don't let this be where the journey ends; let it be where your next level begins.

Acknowledgements

This book is the result of not only my journey but the unwavering support, belief, and generosity of so many incredible people and an incredible, loving divine God.

To my husband: Thank you for being my safe place, my truth-teller, and my steady presence through every twist and turn of this process. Your belief in me never wavered, even when mine did.

To my daughter, Ali: Your help with research and illustrations brought this book to life in such a meaningful way. Watching you use your gifts to support mine is one of the greatest joys of my life.

To my son, Blake: Thank you for your encouragement, humor, and moments of levity as I navigated this process. Your daily calls always came at just the right time.

To the countless friends who've walked alongside me: Thank you for the encouragement, the late-night pep talks, the prayers, and the laughter. You kept me going, even when I questioned myself.

To Cris Cawley and the incredible team at Game Changer Publishing: Thank you for your vision, guidance, and commitment to making this dream a reality. I can't imagine a better team to walk with through this process.

To Nancy Whiting: Thank you for seeing something in me, for opening doors, for creating space, and for encouraging me to step through boldly. Your leadership and belief have made a lasting impact.

To Laura Hamill: Your wisdom and heart have stayed with me. You were the first to teach me that work is about so much more than just the work.

To the beautiful coaches in my life that have deeply impacted my journey: Dr. Renee St Jacque, Dana Grant, and Brooke Hemingway: Thank you for seeing, encouraging, and unlocking my potential. You've each changed the way I move through the world.

To Dr. Claudia Alabiso: Thank you for the countless hours of work on my nervous system and for sharing your light. I am forever changed because of you.

To all the leaders I've worked with over the years: Thank you for trusting me with your stories, your growth, and your hearts. You have shaped this work more than you know.

Most importantly, to God, my light, my love, my power: Thank you for your constant guidance, strength, and compassion. I know I never walk alone.

"Whether you turn to the right or to the left, your ears will hear a voice behind you, saying, 'This is the way; walk in it.'" —Isaiah 30:21

Citations and Resources

1. Alvesson, M., & Willmott, H. (2002). Identity regulation as organizational control: Producing the appropriate individual. *Journal of Management Studies, 39*(5), 619–644. https://doi.org/10.1111/1467-6486.00305

2. Balban, M. Y., Neri, E., Kogon, M. M., Weed, L., Nouriani, B., Jo, B., Holl, G., Zeitzer, J. M., Spiegel, D., & Huberman, A. D. (2023). Brief structured respiration practices enhance mood and reduce physiological arousal. *Cell Reports Medicine, 4*(1), 100895. https://doi.org/10.1016/j.xcrm.2022.100895

3. Bear, M. F., Connors, B. W., & Paradiso, M. A. (2015). *Neuroscience: Exploring the brain* (4th ed.). Wolters Kluwer.

4. Berkeley Well-Being Institute. (n.d.). *Box breathing: What it is & how to do it.* https://www.berkeleywellbeing.com/box-breathing.html

5. Biotechnology Innovation Organization. (2022). *Clinical development success rates and contributing factors 2011–2020.* https://www.bio.org

6. Brown, B. (2010). *The gifts of imperfection: Let go of who you think you're supposed to be and embrace who you are.* Hazelden Publishing.

7. Brown, B. (2013). *Brené Brown on joy and gratitude.* https://grateful.org/resource/brene-brown-on-joy-and-gratitude

8. Brown, B. (2012). *Daring greatly: How the courage to be vulnerable transforms the way we live, love, parent, and lead.* Gotham Books.

9. Child Mind Institute. (2024, June 18). *What is co-regulation?* Retrieved June 23, 2025, from https://childmind.org/article/what-is-co-regulation/

10. Cleveland Clinic. (2022, August 2). *Box breathing: How it works and why it helps*. Cleveland Clinic. https://health.clevelandclinic.org/box-breathing-benefits

11. Creswell, J. D., Pacilio, L. E., Lindsay, E. K., & Brown, K. W. (2014). Brief mindfulness meditation training alters psychological and neuroendocrine responses to social evaluative stress. *Psychoneuroendocrinology, 44*, 1–12. https://doi.org/10.1016/j.psyneuen.2014.02.007

12. Divine, M. (n.d.). *Box breathing technique*. https://www.markdivine.com

13. *Edmondson, A. (1999). Psychological safety and learning behavior in work teams. Administrative Science Quarterly, 44(2), 350–383.* https://doi.org/10.2307/2666999

14. Fowler, J. H., & Christakis, N. A. (2010). Cooperative behavior cascades in human social networks. *Proceedings of the National Academy of Sciences, 107*(12), 5334–5338.

15. Goetz, J. L., Keltner, D., & Simon-Thomas, E. (2010). Compassion: An evolutionary analysis and empirical review. *Psychological Bulletin, 136*(3), 351–374. https://doi.org/10.1037/a0018807

16. Guo, Z., Li, X., Wang, Z., Lu, Z.-L., & Zhang, D. (2023). Underpinning the neurological source of executive function enhancement via transcranial direct current stimulation (tDCS): A systematic review and meta-analysis. *Neuroscience and Biobehavioral Reviews, 147*, 105088. https://doi.org/10.1016/j.neubiorev.2023.105088

17. Hatfield, E., Cacioppo, J. T., & Rapson, R. L. (1994). *Emotional contagion*. Cambridge University Press.

18. Hopper, S. I., Murray, S. L., Ferrara, L. R., & Singleton, J. K. (2019). Effectiveness of diaphragmatic breathing for reducing physiological and psychological stress in adults: A quantitative systematic review.

JBI Database of Systematic Reviews and Implementation Reports, 17(9), 1855–1876. https://doi.org/10.11124/JBISRIR-2017-003848

19. Hougaard, R., Carter, J., & Afton, M. (2021). *Compassionate leadership: How to do hard things in a human way.* Harvard Business Review Press.

20. Jacobsen, K. (2024, July 31). *5 proven visualization techniques to manage anxiety and stress.* Cathartic Space Counseling. Retrieved June 23, 2025, from https://www.catharticspacecounseling.com/blog/proven-visualization-techniques-to-manage-anxiety-and-stress

21. Kabat-Zinn, J. (2005). *Coming to our senses: Healing ourselves and the world through mindfulness.* Hyperion.

22. Karpman, S. B. (1968). Fairy tales and script drama analysis. *Transactional Analysis Bulletin, 7*(26), 39–43.

23. Korn Ferry. (2018). *The self-disruptive leader: Digital-ready research.* https://www.kornferry.com

24. Markman, A. (2018, January 29). *The impossibility of focusing on two things at once.* MIT Sloan Management Review. https://sloanreview.mit.edu/article/the-impossibility-of-focusing-on-two-things-at-once/

25. Martino, J., Pegg, J., & Frates, E. P. (2015). The connection prescription: Using the power of social interactions and the deep desire for connectedness to empower health and wellness. *American Journal of Lifestyle Medicine, 11*(6), 466–475. https://doi.org/10.1177/1559827615608788

26. Maynard, K. (2023, June 1). *Self-compassion: Improve your well-being and quiet your inner critic.* Behavioral Health Partners Blog. University of Rochester Medical Center. Retrieved June 23, 2025, from https://www.urmc.rochester.edu/behavioral-health-partners/bhp-blog/june-2023/self-compassion-improve-your-well-being-and-quiet

27. Mayo Clinic Staff. (n.d.). *Exercise and stress: Get moving to manage stress.* Mayo Clinic. https://www.mayoclinic.org/healthy-lifestyle/stress-management/in-depth/exercise-and-stress/art-20044469

28. McEwen, B. S., & Sapolsky, R. M. (1995). Stress and the brain: From adaptation to disease. *Annual Review of Neuroscience, 18*(1), 227–247. https://doi.org/10.1146/annurev.ne.18.030195.001303

29. McKenna, R. (2017). Composed: The heart and science of leading under pressure. DustJacket Media.

30. McKenna, R. B. (2025). Personal trust and leadership composure. In *WiLD Leaders State of Trust Report.* WiLD Leaders, Inc.

31. McKinsey & Company. (2022). *The State of Organizations 2022.* https://www.mckinsey.com/capabiliti

32. Morgan, J. A., Corrigan, F., & Baune, B. T. (2015). Effects of physical exercise on central nervous system functions: A review of brain region-specific adaptations. Journal of Molecular Psychiatry, 3(1), 3. https://doi.org/10.1186/s40303-015-0010-8

33. National Library of Medicine. (2022). *Why 90% of clinical drugs fail and how to improve it.* https://pmc.ncbi.nlm.nih.gov/articles/PMC9293739/

34. Neff, K. D., & Germer, C. K. (2018). The mindful self-compassion workbook: A proven way to accept yourself, build inner strength, and thrive. Guilford Press.

35. Northrup, C. (2018). *Dodging energy vampires: An empath's guide to evading relationships that drain you and restoring your health and power.* Hay House.

36. Peretti-Hull, S. (2023, July 27). *How smiling helps attain self-regulation from a polyvagal perspective.* SoulSpace Systems. Retrieved June 23, 2025, from https://www.soulspace.systems/post/how-smiling-helps-attain-self-regulation-from-a-polyvagal-perspective

37. Porges, S. W. (2011). *The polyvagal theory: Neurophysiological foundations of emotions, attachment, communication, and self-regulation.* W. W. Norton & Company.

38. Rizzolatti, G., & Craighero, L. (2004). The mirror-neuron system. *Annual Review of Neuroscience, 27*, 169–192. https://doi.org/10.1146/annurev.neuro.27.070203.144230

39. Robinson, B. (2024, March 27). *Anxiety skyrockets to No. 1 issue among American workers, new study shows.* Forbes. https://www.forbes.com/sites/bryanrobinson/2024/03/27/anxiety-skyrockets-to-no-1-issue-among-american-workers-new-study-shows/

40. Reina, D. S., & Reina, M. L. (2006). *Trust and betrayal in the workplace: Building effective relationships in your organization* (2nd ed.). Berrett-Koehler.

41. Rotter, J. B. (1966). Generalized expectancies for internal versus external control of reinforcement. *Psychological Monographs: General and Applied, 80*(1), 1–28. https://doi.org/10.1037/h0092976

42. Sakuragi, S., & Sugiyama, Y. (2006). Effects of daily walking on subjective symptoms, mood, and autonomic nervous function. *Journal of Physiological Anthropology, 25*(4), 281–289. https://doi.org/10.2114/jpa2.25.281

43. Schein, E. H. (2010). *Organizational culture and leadership* (4th ed.). Jossey-Bass.

44. Schroeder, J., & Fishbach, A. (2019). *The impossibility of focusing on two things at once.* MIT Sloan Management Review. https://sloanreview.mit.edu/article/the-impossibility-of-focusing-on-two-things-at-once/

45. Scott, E., & Morin, A. (2023, October 26). *The benefits of journaling for stress management.* Verywell Mind.

https://www.verywellmind.com/the-benefits-of-journaling-for-stress-management-3144611

46. Seligman, M. E. P., Steen, T. A., Park, N., & Peterson, C. (2005). Positive psychology progress: Empirical validation of interventions. *American Psychologist, 60*(5), 410–421. https://doi.org/10.1037/0003-066X.60.5.410

47. Sheppard, C. (2013). Save your drama for your mama: Drama or leadership is a choice. aChoice Publishing.

48. Smith, S. (2018, April 10). *5-4-3-2-1 coping technique for anxiety.* Behavioral Health Partners, University of Rochester Medical Center. https://www.urmc.rochester.edu/behavioral-health-partners/bhp-blog/april-2018/5-4-3-2-1-coping-technique-for-anxiety

49. Song, C., Ikei, H., & Miyazaki, Y. (2016). Physiological effects of nature therapy: A review of the research in Japan. *International Journal of Environmental Research and Public Health, 13*(8), 781. https://doi.org/10.3390/ijerph13080781

50. Southwick, S. M., & Charney, D. S. (2018). *Resilience: The science of mastering life's greatest challenges* (2nd ed.). Cambridge University Press.

51. Taneja, A. (2014). *The neuroscience of smiling: How facial expressions affect brain chemistry.* Psychology Today. https://www.psychologytoday.com/us/blog/your-brain-work/201403/the-neuroscience-smiling

52. University of California, Davis Health. (2022, December). *10 health benefits of meditation and how to focus on mindfulness and compassion.* Cultivating Health Blog. Retrieved June 23, 2025, from https://health.ucdavis.edu/blog/cultivating-health/10-health-benefits-of-meditation-and-how-to-focus-on-mindfulness-and-compassion/2022/12

53. University of Rochester Medical Center. (n.d.). *Co-regulation.* In URMC Health Encyclopedia. Retrieved June 23, 2025, from https://www.urmc.rochester.edu/encyclopedia/content?ContentID=4552&ContentTypeID=1

54. WiLD Leaders. (2025). *State of Trust Report.* WiLD Leaders, Inc. https://www.wildleaders.org

55. Zahn, R., Lythe, K. E., Gethin, J. A., Green, S., Deakin, J. F., Young, A. H., & Moll, J. (2009). The role of self-esteem in the moral judgment of emotions. *Social Cognitive and Affective Neuroscience, 4*(3), 371–378. https://doi.org/10.1093/scan/nsp020

THANK YOU FOR READING MY BOOK!

I WOULD LOVE TO CONNECT!

Scan the QR Code:

I appreciate your interest in my book and value your feedback, as it helps me improve future versions. I would be so grateful if you would leave your invaluable review on Amazon.com and help me spread the word. Thank you!

www.ingramcontent.com/pod-product-compliance
Lightning Source LLC
Chambersburg PA
CBHW030247010526
44107CB00031B/1350/J